Hase of Japan

(the story of Koshi Hasegawa)

by
SOLVEIG SMITH

Salvationist Publishing and Supplies Ltd.,
Judd Street, King's Cross, London WC1H 9NN

© The Salvation Army 1975
First Published 1975
ISBN 0 85412 270 2

Mrs. Commissioner Smith
is a Salvation Army officer who has served in India, Burma, Great Britain, Pakistan and Japan. She is now serving in her native land, Denmark, where her husband, Commissioner Don Smith, is the Territorial Commander. She is the author of several books including *In An Indian Garden* and *East is East*.

MADE AND PRINTED IN GREAT BRITAIN BY
THE CAMPFIELD PRESS, ST. ALBANS, HERTS.

CONTENTS

Chapter		*Page*
	PROLOGUE	1
1.	FORESHADOW OF THINGS TO COME	14
2.	CHANGES	22
3.	FROM NAVY TO ARMY	33
4.	CHO THE BUTTERFLY	43
5.	THE BUTTERFLY SPREADS HER WINGS	52
6.	HASEGAWA CATCHES THE BUTTERFLY	62
7.	HASEGAWA AS HUSBAND AND FATHER	69
8.	WAR CLOUDS GATHER	78
9.	RAVAGES OF WAR AND RESTORATION	88
10.	AS AMBASSADOR	99
11.	AS AN EVANGELIST	110

PROLOGUE
A COUNTRY AND A PEOPLE

Is it possible for one of a different cultural background to write with understanding about a Japanese, an Occidental to grasp the inner thoughts and aspirations of an Oriental? To try to portray the character of a man of a race different from one's own may be no easy task, yet I have an overwhelming desire to record the things I have learned and heard and seen in the nearly four years my husband and I were privileged to live in Japan, and the even shorter time we had the good fortune to know Commissioner Koshi Hasegawa.

The Japanese are not an easily understood people; at least, such is popular opinion. The reasons are various. For centuries Japan was a closed country; a group of islands on the world's perimeter, isolated, remote, developing a tradition and culture of their own, borrowed in the dim distant past from the Asian mainland; a single race, speaking one language, following the same pattern of living—a homogeneous entity. As a result many Japanese, even today, feel uneasy with members of other nations. Having a code of conduct not shared generally by other people, they find difficulty in knowing how to behave in the presence of 'foreigners', or how to accept them. It is salutary for those who belong to the Occidental races to remember that the western pattern of life is not the only one, neither is it necessarily the best.

Francis Xavier wrote home from Japan in the middle of the sixteenth century: 'The Japanese are people of very good manners, good in general, and not malicious; they are men of honour to a marvel, and prize honour above all else in the world.'

The western world has attributed a certain mysticism

to the people of the East, an inscrutability hard to penetrate. James Clark Moloney in *Understanding the Japanese Mind* says: ' My conviction is that its people are neither " mysterious ", " inscrutable " nor " unpredictable ", but that they are, in fact, entirely reasonable, understandable, and predictable when one fully understands the restrictions which have been placed upon their behaviour, individual and collective, by the traditions of the ages.' I share his view.

Circumstances and conditions in which one is forced to live play a big part in moulding the character and characteristics of a people. Even the contour of a country sets a stamp on its inhabitants. Living on a string of relatively small islands, over-populated and crammed together owing to the mountainous nature of the country, has undoubtedly placed its mark on the Japanese and developed certain reflexes and immunities different from those of a people with more *lebensraum*. By force of circumstances they have learnt to live together, to move around in crowds, yet to honour each other's privacy; to be courteous and polite (except when having to push their way in and out of local transport); to cut off the rest of the world on arriving in their little homes where they recline on *tatami* (straw mats) floors behind glazed windows.

Only 12 per cent of the total area of Japan is cultivated, or even cultivable. Wherever one travels, from Hokkaido in the north through Honshu and Shikoku to Kyushu in the south, mountains form the main structure of the landscape: the mountains of Hokkaido, snow-clad in winter, and glowing with autumn colours of bronze and gold maple and wild vines in the fall; the mountains of Honshu and the islands of the Inland Sea, purple-hued, wreathed in veils of mist like famous paintings on ancient scrolls; and the mountains of sub-tropical Kyushu, which include the world's largest volcano, Mount Aso, its awesome craters spreading over a distance of 80 kilometres.

Most beloved and revered of all is Fuji-San, or Fuji-Yama (Fuji mountain), on which Her Imperial Highness the Empress of Japan composed a verse for the 1972 annual poetry recital held in the imperial palace. The style is classical 'haiku', consisting of seventeen syllables:

> Far beyond the blue sea
> The sacred mountain of Fuji
> Towered white with snow
> Shimmering in the morning glow.

These few choice words reveal to the Japanese mind a whole landscape of beauty and excite deep feelings of reverence and awe. Mount Fuji's fame lies not in its height, rising to 12,390 ft., but in its unique, almost perfect symmetrical cone-like shape. It stands alone like a sentinel, keeping watch over a hundred million people, majestic, unassailable, serene and calm from without, yet a suppressed force of energy within. Although lying sixty miles west of Tokyo, Fuji-San can, under favourable conditions, be seen from certain parts of the city. Occasionally we saw it on early morning walks, when the rays of the rising sun touched it with gold. It was always an inspiration for us, living in a crowded, smoke-filled city, to look upon such purity and perfection of form.

Traditionally, Mount Fuji arose from the earth in a single night, about 300 BC, while Lake Biwa, near Kyoto, sank simultaneously. An interesting fact is that volcanic mountains are still arising from the earth in Japan. As recently as July 1944 an eruption took place in Hokkaido. Where before were fertile fields, now stands a 400-metre-high volcanic mountain. It is called Showa Shinzan. Showa implies the present period in which it came into being, and Shinzan means 'new mountain'. From its bowels is emitted sulphuretted smoke, a sight both fascinating and awe-inspiring, yet frightening and eerie.

Wherever you travel in Japan you are aware of nature's

forces. Hot springs spurt from under the ground and steam rises in columns to the sky. Even the earth trembles! From time immemorial Japan has been an earth-shaken land. The residents of the country have to learn to live with this, always hoping that the movement will remain only a tremor. The flimsily-built houses of unpainted light wood and rice paper screens, typical Japanese homes before earthquake-proof foundations were thought of, must have been modelled with earthquakes in mind. Kamo no Chomei of the twelfth century wrote: ' Only in a hut built for the moment can one live without fears.' For the moment! The moment has great importance to the Japanese, so much of their restless energy has to be crammed into it. Is it because they live with the transience of things around them, that they want to make the most of the present? Life is uncertain, and if death comes, well, it comes; this is the one certainty in life, so why mourn it?

I dislike crowds, yet when caught up in a swarm of fast-moving people on a Tokyo station there is something fascinating, something exhilarating about the experience. They are so alive, so bursting with energy, like their volcanic mountains. To watch the Japanese at work always brings pleasure. They look as though they are really enjoying it! Whether road-workers, labourers on a building site, or individuals on a special job in the house, they put zest into all they do, like the man who came to fix our oil-heater one winter. Without stopping for lunch (or a smoke), he worked from 11 a.m. to 4 p.m., taking the whole mechanism to pieces, placing each item neatly on a cloth, putting each back painstakingly with the precision and skill of an artist. When the task was completed, he took the trouble politely to tell me how often oil should be ordered, marking the dates on my calendar, so that the tank would not run dry.

The Japanese work long hours, 48 to 55 hours a week

with only one Saturday free in a month. Their attitude to work is remarkable; they relish it and find great satisfaction in trying to do it to perfection. They are fairly well paid nowadays and, as they do not spend a great deal on their homes, apart from electrical equipment obtained quite cheaply, money is available for travelling, a new and popular luxury to the present-day Japanese.

They journey in groups to Europe and America anxious to learn about other people and to be accepted into the brotherhood of man by other nations. We can learn much from this vital race, always on the move, yet calm; calm and serene like Mount Fuji, with an inner force continually driving them on. This idea of harnessed energy or disciplined force is also exemplified in their great art of flower cultivation and formal landscape gardens. The bonsai (dwarf trees) are shaped by trimming, pruning and wiring, ' embodying an ideal of human conduct, a compromise between the forces of life and anti-life. The little tree flourishes without any sign of conflict, fulfilling its purpose of existence by giving forth flowers for the delight of man, teaching man the art of living within limitations imposed by the environment' (in *Japan Times*, by Martin C. Davidson).

The formal landscape gardens bespeak a similar order and discipline; every stone and rock is carefully chosen and placed in relation to streams, shrubs and trees. But when one sees chrysanthemums trained by tiny wire racks inserted in each flower to keep them in place, we, who are more for letting nature take its course, may be tempted to look upon this as too much of a good thing.

The ' tea ceremony ', another aspect of Japanese culture and tradition, teaches the same principle. In an article in the magazine *PHP*, Sushitsu Sen states that in the tea ceremony one experiences the effect of order and learns the relevance of this order to freedom and peace of mind.

It would seem that within the framework of discipline and order they find security, and in team work they find strength.

So these forms of cultural heritage, as well as the structure of their country, have set an indelible stamp on the people; inwardly passionate, kept in control by discipline and restraint, for self-respect always means restraint to a Japanese. Outwardly they are proud, aloof and with an innate dignity; inwardly affectionate and capable of deep feeling and friendship.

Other examples of this discipline and order are found in everyday life. When the 'bullet train', the fastest in the world, with a speed of 210 kilometres per hour, comes to a halt at a station, each door of the train is at the very point where queues of travellers stand waiting in their allotted places. Within three minutes the crowds have entered, found their seats and the train is off. Hardly ever is any train late in Japan. Should an express not get its passengers to their destination on time, money is refunded!

The same discipline and order is seen in the school children with knapsacks on their backs, containing pockets for this and that, hooks for umbrellas and little bags for keys; a place for everything and everything in its place. Similarly, on the streets after a rainshower, men stand meticulously folding each pleat of their collapsible umbrellas.

Etiquette in daily behaviour is adhered to with equal thoroughness. The choice of colour in women's clothing is regulated by age. Only the young are seen in bright colours; as the years go by the red and pink is changed to green and brown, and with advancing years to grey and black. Finally, on passing her sixtieth birthday, a woman is free from convention and in a happy 'second childhood' has the privilege of reverting to wearing red.

One Christmas when I called to see some friends, they

handed me a gift. It was a beautiful set of Japanese *gheta* (sandals) with matching handbag in bright red and gold. I was naturally delighted, but when our Japanese travelling companion, who knew my age, saw the set he said apologetically, ' They thought you could wear it, but they were mistaken.' I had still a little time longer to wait for freedom from formality!

Saying ' thank you ' and ' pardon me ' is never neglected in Japan. ' *Sumimasen* ' (pardon me) recurs so frequently that the foreigner often wonders what there may be to pardon. Every act of courtesy or kindness must be acknowledged; a gift received is reciprocated by another gift, though not more expensive than the one received, to avoid causing embarrassment to the original giver. It is all very complicated to the uninitiated, as I soon found out!

One Sunday when accompanying my husband to one of our Salvation Army centres in Tokyo, I was approached by an elderly woman who thanked me for dedicating her grandson on a previous visit to Hokkaido, where her daughter and son-in-law are engaged in Salvation Army work. She then presented me with an enormous bag of roasted peanuts. We like peanuts, but this seemed a mammoth quantity to eat. As it happened we had a friend with us from another part of the world, who would not feel any embarrassment in sharing our peanuts; but that was not the end. The following day my husband came home from the office with a still larger parcel of peanuts— salted peanuts, shelled peanuts and unshelled peanuts. Evidently the appreciative woman had felt obliged to express her gratitude for blessings received through my husband's sermon, and this was her way. But who would help us through this mountain of peanuts now? I thought of our able translator with his family. After all, he knew from whence the peanuts had come and would not feel under any obligation in receiving a share. In good faith I sent him some. The next day I received from him a tin of tea in return for our peanuts!

When remonstrating gently with him, I said: ' You knew where the peanuts came from, you knew I had not bought them, so surely there was no need for you to give us something in return?' He smiled and replied: ' You shared your peanuts and I share with you my tea which *I didn't pay for either*!' The circle of kindnesses and obligations is never broken.

One of the unusual customs of gift-giving, unusual at least to visitors from overseas, is at weddings. The bride and bridegroom not only receive gifts; they also give gifts to each of the wedding guests. Every gift is beautifully wrapped and tied, however many guests are present. It is a common sight to see people who have attended a wedding leave the reception carrying their gift in a *furoshiki* (a silk or nylon square used as a wrapper).

But the most beautiful and surprising gift I ever received from Japanese friends was one for which I am still indebted. When word went round that we were leaving Japan to take an appointment in Denmark, the country in which I was born, I received a delightful bouquet of flowers sent from a Japanese lady I had met only once. The flowers were those that grow in Danish fields in summertime, marguerites, daisies, cornflowers, poppies, and with them were sheaves of ripe golden corn. They appeared so real that when friends in Copenhagen saw them and I said I had brought them from Japan, they looked disbelievingly at me. Every flower petal and every leaf, yes, even to the stamen and the ears of corn, were made with such precision that the finished product was completely lifelike. Cloth had been treated with individual dyes to secure the exact shade of colour for each article, then cut and shaped to perfection. Attention to detail is a pronounced Japanese characteristic. The giver of this particular gift, a master in the art of flower-making, travels the world lecturing, and displaying her great art. Why she should have taken the trouble and time to make these flowers for me, and how I can ever repay her kindness, I do not know. At least, it gives perfect proof that behind a façade of apparent aloofness is hidden a wealth of human sympathy and kindness.

The Japanese, on the whole, cannot be classed as a religious people. Perhaps their restless energy denies them the time to sit and fathom theological questions or meditate on spiritual truths. One does not find an attitude of worship and devotion in their temples or shrines as seen in similar places in other countries of the East. It may well be that for the majority in Japan facts are more easily understood than faith. They are, however, an upright people, with a high sense of honesty. An announcement in the *Japan Times* intrigued me. It stated that during the last fiscal year the amount of lost cash on Japan National Railways topped the 1,000 million yen mark. The bulk of this was returned to the owners, but there was still 100,560,000 which after six months without claimants became absorbed as ' miscellaneous income ' for the JNR. Could that happen in any other country?

A letter from a visitor to Tokyo sent to the *Japan Times* is also worth quoting: ' Recently I passed through Tokyo with my wife and two children on our way to the U.S.A. from Hong Kong. While travelling in a taxi from the airport to the Azabu Prince Hotel I removed my suit coat. When later we left the taxi the coat was left behind. As the coat contained our four passports and airline tickets, you can imagine our dismay when we realized what had happened soon after the taxi had departed. The staff of the Azabu Prince Hotel was most sympathetic and spent the entire afternoon trying, unsuccessfully, to locate the taxi. Real credit then goes to the helpful taxi driver, who apologetically returned four hours later after having only just discovered my coat on the back shelf of his car.'

As personal experiences may be even more convincing than quotes, I will add one or two.

Baby John, son of a British couple who have worked in Japan for many years, on going to town with his mother and me, lost his Teddy bear; a loss discovered after we were seated in the bus. I felt sure he hadn't had it when getting into the vehicle. The mother was not worried; she had lived in Japan long enough to know that anything lost would be found and, if at all possible, returned. When walking home from the bus stop, hours later, we saw the bear sitting in a local shop window, looking out for his owner. The woman in the shop said to the mother when she claimed it: ' It was brought in from the street where someone found it. I hoped you would see it.' Only a dropped Teddy bear, yet it revealed Japanese thoughtfulness in picking it up and making sure it would be returned to the child who had lost it! Few are tempted to pocket a Teddy bear, but 5,000 yen is a lot of money, and this the woman, who came to our house every month with the electricity bill, returned when I had inadvertently given her too much.

Our neighbour lost her watch somewhere when shopping one day and decided the loss must have occurred in taking off her gloves in a department store. On phoning and inquiring, she was told someone had found a watch on the floor and handed it in. Would she come and claim it? She would!

These are but a few experiences of a country and a people as I personally found them. Many writers have made a comprehensive study of Japan; I make no such claim, but write of what I have seen and heard, hoping to give an idea of Koshi Hasegawa's background, for this was the country which he loved and these were the people whose traditions shaped his life and whose aspirations he shared.

*   *   *

PROLOGUE

We were on our way to the Evangeline Hall in downtown Tokyo. It was Friday night of November 6, 1970. My husband was driving the car. Mrs. Commissioner Hasegawa, wife of the Territorial Counsellor, was in the back seat, chatting with her usual high spirits, about wind and weather in an amusing mixture of Japanese and English.

An ambulance approached us from the opposite side, rending the air with its frightening, foreboding siren. The traffic was held up for a moment—then the ambulance was gone. Our conversation stopped; the evening air suddenly felt chilly.

Minutes later we reached our destination and noticed people congregating outside the hall in greater numbers than usual. As the united holiness meeting was soon to commence, the crowd seemed natural enough. We stepped out of the car and at once realized that something unusual had happened. The atmosphere was charged with tragedy. Quietly and sympathetically we were told by one of the officers that Commissioner Hasegawa, while crossing the road in front of the hall, had been knocked down by a car and taken to the nearest hospital in the ambulance that had just passed us. Immediately we inquired the whereabouts of the hospital and an officer came with us in the car to direct us to it.

When we arrived, the Commissioner was already being examined and we were asked to wait in the entrance hall of the casualty department. I looked at Mrs. Hasegawa. What could I say to comfort her? She took the shock so bravely. When I suggested that she telephone her son she replied calmly: ' If bad, then I phone; if not bad, then I not give trouble.' With the inbred precept of her country, never to inflict your own troubles on others, she remained calm and composed.

So we waited and watched the people coming and

going, taking off their shoes and putting on slippers when entering the hospital and reversing the procedure on leaving. A couple of policemen came to investigate the seriousness of the Commissioner's accident; they too donned slippers.

Eventually we were called to one of the private rooms. We suggested that perhaps Mrs. Hasegawa would like to see her husband alone first, but she beckoned us to go with her. When we entered the room we found the Commissioner with his head bandaged, but with a tranquil smile on his face. He even tried to sit up, then apologized, again and again, for causing such trouble and upsetting the plans for the holiness meeting he had hoped to attend.

Greatly relieved that his injuries were not worse, we fully expected that after some weeks the two gashes sustained in the head would heal. It was typical of the Commissioner to make light of his serious condition; he even joked about it when visitors came to see him, saying that being unconscious was the most comfortable feeling he had ever experienced, like floating on a soft cloud with all his anxieties and cares left behind.

Commissioner Hasegawa did not make the recovery for which we all had hoped. Never robust and of recent years failing in health, the loss of blood was too great for his frail frame and, within a few days, his long and illustrious life drew to a close. He died as he had lived—peacefully and confidently. The Power that had sustained him in life sustained him also through the gates of death into life eternal.

There was little outward expression of sorrow; the Japanese consider it improper to embarrass others with their tears. Mrs. Hasegawa showed marvellous composure throughout the many services held for her husband. Only once did she give way to her personal grief and for a moment put her head on my shoulder and shed a tear when I called with flowers at the home she had shared with him for so many years.

Apologetically she smiled through her tears and said: ' Now I won't ever again hear his voice calling out as he used to when he came home: " *Tadaima* " (I am back).'

Chapter One

FORESHADOW OF THINGS TO COME

KOSHI HASEGAWA, born at the turn of the century in a small village, in Hyogo Prefecture, near the seaport of Kobe, on the south-eastern coast of Japan, was a son of the village *Shoya*. As head of a part of the community, the father looked after village property; decided the days for co-operative work in the fields, in house-building and road-repair; accepted responsibility for ensuring the villagers' good behaviour; reported to Government any crime; and announced the dates for local holidays by going around the streets beating together two blocks of wood in a certain rhythm.

Of the nine children in the family, five boys and four girls, Koshi was the seventh, with two sisters younger than himself.

Endowed with good looks and a gentle nature, Hasegawa was in his seventieth year when I heard a Chinese officer say, in great admiration: ' You are the most handsome Japanese I have ever met! ' His hair was then snowy white, his slim frame erect, his eyes gentle and wise. He had a distinguished appearance, a regal bearing commanding respect, yet he was also lovable, his presence always bringing an atmosphere of harmony and peace.

Koshi had a happy childhood, like most Japanese children; he was loved and cherished by his family. He was a thoughtful child, fond of birds and flowers, and spent many joyous moments picking wild flowers in the

FORESHADOW OF THINGS TO COME

fields or by the wayside. Having gathered a pretty bunch, he would run home and hand the bouquet to his mother with a grin on his boyish face. Mother understood the meaning of that look, for he was fond of her. Between the two lay a special bond of affection.

She was of a gentle and compassionate nature, and her temperament was passed on to her son. All through life her influence upon him remained strong. He often spoke of her with profound reverence for her high qualities of honesty and integrity. In name she remained Buddhist till death on November 26, 1945. She was given a Buddhist funeral, yet her last words were: 'Always put your trust in God and not in man.'

Koshi had great respect for his father. In those days it was accepted custom for a household to look upon the father as the chief authority; his words were law and indisputable. An old Japanese saying, *'Jishin, Kaminari, Kagi, Oyaji ga taihen kowai mono desu'* can be rendered, ' Earthquake, lightning, fire and father are to be feared '. Although it did not go to such extremes in the Hasegawa household, every morning Koshi bowed before his father and addressed him with the traditional greeting: ' *Ohayo gozaimasu* ' (polite form for ' Good morning '; literally, ' You are early ').

Discipline and order were instilled into the children, not so much by scolding or threat as by their parents' and elders' patient repetition and example in the home. Use of slippers, second nature to any Japanese, is proof of how example shown over and over again creates habit, so that any Japanese youngster follows the rule, quite instinctively, of taking off shoes, putting on slippers at the entrance to the house, leaving the slippers outside when entering the *tatami* room, where the family sleeps on the straw-mat floor, and again changing into special slippers provided for the water closet. It is very complicated for a new visitor to Japan who invariably finds himself walking round in the wrong slippers, or feeling cold about the feet and wondering why!

Koshi, like any other Japanese child, was also taught '*jicho*', self-respect—never to do anything that would bring shame on himself or on the family name—and that he had obligations toward his family and the outside world. As yet the responsibilities of life did not weigh heavily upon him; he was still living in a child's world of freedom and fancy, spending the hours by the little stream near the house, lying on his back looking up at the blue sky, watching the birds in flight, fancying himself a bird flying over mountains and valleys, or over great cities and the deep tempestuous sea. In his mind's eye he pictured it all. He would listen to the wind in the grass, and the insects' chirping, and the gentle tinkle of the '*furin*', a little metal bell hanging in a branch of a tree near the house, sounding every time the wind stirred the prayer paper attached to it. He passed the time making paper boats, setting them on the water to glide down the stream, imagining they would reach the ocean and sail on to strange and exciting places round the world. The dream of a child was a foreshadowing of things to come; in the child's imagination were the still unformed ambitions that were later to shape his life.

One incident that stood out from his early childhood, and which he later related to his son and daughters, was the day he fell down from the pomegranate tree. It was a warm day in early autumn when the pomegranates hung full and red and ripe from the branches of a tree behind the family house. Koshi looked at the fruit, so tempting, but beyond his reach. He climbed up the slender trunk, hung on to a branch, and stretched for a pomegranate. There was a crunch, the branch broke off, and down fell Koshi with a bang. His mother, busy in the kitchen, heard the thud and came running. She found the boy dazed and bruised. A rickshaw was called to take him to

FORESHADOW OF THINGS TO COME

a doctor living some distance away. He examined Koshi's limbs and sore head, assured the mother that nothing was broken, admonished the boy to refrain from anything so foolish in future, and bandaged him up.

Jogging along on the way home Koshi was torn between two feelings: he loved the adventure of riding in a rickshaw but felt terribly embarrassed because of his swathed head. Like all Japanese children, he had early been warned never to put himself in a position of ridicule or embarrassment, and he felt it was *infra dig* to show himself to all and sundry with a bandaged head.

In Koshi's home, typical of most Japanese homes, were two shrines, a Buddhist and a Shinto. The Buddhist shrine was the more important, with pictures or tablets on which were engraved the names of deceased family members. Each day fresh flowers or branches of a certain tree and an offering of food were placed before it. Often Koshi heard his mother speaking to his ancestors, informing them of family events. The little light around the shrine gave a comforting glow through dark nights, and sweet-smelling incense filled the air.

The Shinto shrine, of lesser importance, received scant attention. On festive days Koshi, dressed in his best clothes, was taken, with the rest of the family, to the *jinja* (Shinto) temple. Excitedly he looked forward to the outing, not so much because of the religious aspect as for the treat he and his brothers and sisters received in sweets and special food. A spirit of gaiety surrounded the whole affair; women in bright-coloured kimonos flitted about on wooden *getas* looking like magnified butterflies. All were in festive mood; even the worshippers seemed to take their devotions lightly. After summoning the gods by a swift clapping of hands, bowing their heads for a minute or two, clapping their hands again in dismissal, throwing coins in a well, they then went off to enjoy themselves buying *omikuji* (lottery from the gods)—hoping for a word of good luck. Vendors, having set up stalls at the entrance to the shrine, were busy supplying customers with food, drinks and souvenirs.

The idea of adhering to both the Shinto and Buddhist religion may seem strange. To say, however, that most Japanese believe in both would not be correct. That a majority of the Japanese people pay respect to both Shinto and Buddhist rituals is nearer the truth. In Hasegawa's childhood these were observed more strictly, for in Japan, as in many other countries, religious practices are on the wane; but even today, during ground-breaking ceremonies for ultra-modern factories and high-rise buildings, Shinto priests in ancient-style costumes are present to give their blessing. Weddings are solemnized before Shinto altars, while funerals are conducted according to Buddhist rites. A new-born child is taken by its parents to the Shinto shrine to be blessed with health and long life, while at home mother worships daily before the Buddhist shrine. Both Shintoism and Buddhism are given allegiance seemingly without conflicting loyalties. In the Japanese mind there is no inconsistency in this duality; the two blend in relative concord.

Shinto, literally 'the way of the gods', is the name given to the mythology and to the ancestor and nature worship which preceded the coming of Buddhism to Japan from India. Shinto can, in fact, hardly be called a religion, its gods are like those of Greek mythology; it has no clear dogma, no sacred book, no moral code.

When in the middle of the sixth-century Buddhism arrived in Japan via China, it mingled with Shintoism, neither repelling the other, except for a short time after inception.

Kyozo Mori San, adviser to one of Japan's leading newspapers, throws light on this strange union in an article in the magazine *PHP*, giving several reasons for the harmonious mixture: one, ' because Shintoism was primarily based on rituals and had no founder or doctrine, therefore no struggles on dogma '; two, ' Buddhism is a religion of peaceful co-existence '; three, ' the Buddhist priests made efforts to reconcile their propagation activities with the traditional Japanese thought regarding gods. The common people accepted Shintoism and Buddhism as something like two sides of a coin.'

While the ordinary days of the year passed in pleasant monotony in Koshi's childhood, festive days and holidays stood out like coloured shells on a seashore of sand. New Year was the biggest festival of all, a time of general merry-making. For weeks before the day, mother busily cleaned the house, turning out useless articles and decorating the front entrance with *kado-matsu* and *shime-nawa*. *Kado-matsu* is an arrangement of pine, plum and bamboo seen outside every house in Japan during New Year. The pine symbolizes long life due to its hardiness, the bamboo stem constancy, and the plum virtue. Amid the decorations are placed fern leaves, an orange and a small lobster, representing good wishes for a long, strong and prosperous life. *Shime-nawa*, also called the taboo-rope, is slung across the top of the entrance to the house with tufts of straw and strips of white paper, supposedly to keep evil spirits from entering the house in the New Year.

As the midnight hour struck, Koshi heard the temple bell ringing out the sins of the world. One hundred and eight times it chimed and for each chime a sin was cancelled until the last chime was heard and the human race could start afresh with a clean record.

When the first day of the year dawned everyone was happy and the family sat on cushions by the low table, mother serving special dishes such as rice-cakes and vegetables together with other delicacies—herring roe, black beans, dried chestnuts, seaweeds and lotus roots. Each dish is of special significance. Chestnuts denoted success in the New Year; the word for chestnut in Japanese, is *katchiguri*. *Katchi*, means 'victory or triumph'. The lotus root stands for purity, as by Buddhists the lotus is considered a sacred plant, growing in muddy water, yet its upward stem bears white, pure flowers.

Gifts were exchanged by family members and as children in other countries look forward to Christmas gifts, so Koshi and his brothers and sisters looked forward to this day with great anticipation. Friends and neighbours called and were entertained; the house was filled with friendly chatter for four or five days, while the children played in the background, stuffing themselves with *mochi* (flat, round rice-cakes) without which no New Year in Japan would be complete.

While this was a family festival enjoyed by all, there was another festival to which Koshi and his four brothers particularly looked forward because it was especially for them. It was observed every year on May 5 and called 'Boys' Day'. Mother again busily decorated the house and cooked special dishes for the occasion. This time iris leaves were placed on the eaves of the house to keep it free of evil spirits.

Iris leaves were also used to wrap the special dumplings called *chimaki*, which the boys ate to their hearts' content. The reason why the iris flower is so prominent in this festival is that it blooms at this time of the year and the name of the festival in Japanese is *Shobu-no-sekku*—the festival of the iris. This flower, with its long, narrow leaf resembling a sword, signifies striving for success, and can probably be traced back to the Samurai, the warriors of Japan, whose traditional badge of office was a sword.

The most exciting part of the festival, however, was hoisting colourful cloth streamers in the shape of carp on a tall bamboo pole in the garden and watching them 'swimming' in the air like fish. One carp was hoisted for each boy in the family. How proud were the Hasegawas of their five carp on top of the bamboo pole for all to see!

FORESHADOW OF THINGS TO COME

Each year father explained to his sons that just as the carp has energy and strength to fight its way up swift-running streams, cascades and waterfalls, so he wanted them to develop strength of character and will-power to overcome all obstacles in life, to be brave and courageous. On Koshi's sensitive young mind, this made a lasting impression.

Chapter
Two

CHANGES

WHILE Koshi was spending his childhood years in the happy and peaceful seclusion of his village home, tremendous changes were taking place in the country. Little did he know then how he would be caught up in the turbulent transitions and how those changes would affect his own life.

For more than two centuries Japan had been a closed country and all foreigners kept out. Any Japanese venturing abroad paid for the adventure with his life if he returned home. Then, in the mid-nineteenth century a change took place. In 1853 Commodore Matthew C. Perry, of the United States Navy, sailed into Tokyo Bay. America wanted Japan to open her ports for America's ships to take water and replenish stores and coal. A letter from the President of the United States was handed to the ruler of Japan demanding inauguration of trade relations.

' The Japanese were appalled by the size and guns of the American " black ships ", as they called them, and they were amazed by the steam-powered vessels which moved up the bay against the wind. They realized that their own shore batteries were almost useless against the American warships, before which Edo (the capital) lay defenceless' (*Japan, Past and Present*, by Edwin O. Reischauer, p. 110).

An agreement was signed and with that a door to the outside world opened, however reluctantly. But once open no one could stem the powerful influence that swept the country and the changes that inevitably followed.

Japan has always had an Emperor. The earliest record

of an enthronement goes back as far as 660 BC, though for many centuries the Emperor was solely the symbol of religion, the Shinto high priest of ancient Yamato tradition, the sacred head of the nation. Affairs of State were in the hands of feudal lords, known as *daimyo*, and above these the Shogun, the military generalissimo.

In 1868 the Shogun voluntarily surrendered actual rule of the country to the Emperor, a forward-looking and vigorous young man, who then officially assumed direct jurisdiction over the nation. His rule, lasting from 1868 to 1912, brought about what is known as the Meiji restoration, a period which transformed Japan from an isolated, insignificant country to a vital modern nation.

Among many changes the Emperor transferred his court from Kyoto and set up the imperial capital in Edo, which he renamed Tokyo, meaning the ' Eastern capital '. Today Tokyo is the largest city in the world, with eleven million inhabitants.

With the feudal system abolished there came also an end of the Samurai class: the feudal retainers, warrior-administrators, the hierarchy of the four social classes of Japanese society. No longer were they allowed their traditional badge of office, the two swords, one long and the other short, which a Samurai, for centuries, had proudly worn at his side.

No longer did Japan believe in isolation. The doors were flung wide open. From the narrow enclosure of national boundaries the eyes of the nation were lifted to the wide horizon of the whole world. Envoys and students were sent abroad to learn the skills of the Occident. For them the world had become a vast schoolroom, and with Japanese thoroughness they set about learning from each country that in which it specifically excelled. They observed, they assimilated, and often improved upon the original. They desired to make Japan a strong nation like the leading Western powers and they looked to the West for a new pattern of society and government. They noted and learnt from the powerful nations, alas, to their own eventual downfall, that military strength was needed to annex new territory. Overseas expansion and colonial possessions were the mark of prestige and power. National military service was introduced.

The Western calendar was also adopted, and the months given numbers: January—1st month, February—2nd month and so on, but they still retained the old system of counting the year from the enthronement of the ruling Emperor. The current era is called 'Showa', the Emperor having, up to the present time of writing, ruled 50 years. This year is Showa 50 (AD 1975). This system necessitates some speedy mental arithmetic when Japanese and foreigners compare dates. A happening, say in 1925, may be referred to. That date means nothing to the Japanese. To 'translate' it into his own era he must quickly subtract 25 from 75 to ascertain how many years ago it happened—50 years—that would be the first year of the Showa era. But what if the previous year AD 1924 was referred to? That would be in the previous era and one would have to know how many years the previous Emperor had ruled to calculate the date. Presumably the Japanese must know exactly how many years each Emperor ruled, for if you ask any Japanese what year in their calculation AD 1924 is, he would after a slight hesitation smilingly tell you 'Taisho 15'. The previous Emperor ruled fifteen years! The end of an era concludes with the death of an Emperor and the new era commences the same year with the enthronement of the new Emperor.

There is another complicated system which, fortunately, has fallen out of use. In calculating one's age, the Japanese consider the calendar year rather than the exact number of years or months. If a person is born in November he will be one until the 31st of December of that year, and considered two years old in January of the following year, even though he is in reality only two months old. The same would apply to anyone born on the 31st of December, the baby would be two years old when but two days! In 1950 (Showa 25!) the Diet decided that the Western way of counting age should be brought into use, though many of the old school still persist that a child is one the day of his birth. But gradually things are changing and the old gives way to the new.

To make the nation literate a most ambitious educational scheme was embarked upon. Thousands of school buildings were erected and tens of thousands of teachers trained. Primary schooling, commencing at the age of six, became compulsory for all. In a short time Japan scored as the first Asian country to have a literate people, in spite of the fact that written Japanese is probably the most difficult of all languages. It shares no fewer than 3,000 characters with the Chinese language and out of these, 1,865 must be learnt in order to be able to read the daily papers. Beside these the Japanese language has two other alphabets, Hiragana and Katagana, both with forty-six letters or signs, which are rather reminiscent of shorthand script. Most books are written in a mixture of Chinese characters (called Kanji) and Hiragana, with Katagana for any foreign words that might occur. The Chinese characters convey the nouns and stems of words, while the Hiragana signs serve to transcribe particles and terminations.

From the beginning equal opportunity for education was given to both girls and boys; the elementary schools then established throughout the country were attended by children of both sexes, irrespective of class distinction. An imperial rescript inaugurating the scheme read: ' Henceforth education shall be so diffused that there shall be no ignorant family in the land and no family with an ignorant member.'

This manifesto did much to help Japan toward the tremendous progress achieved within the last century, and has made her people the most literate nation in the world.

To a westerner Japanese ideographs are complicated and one is inclined to feel pity for the children of Japan, but who knows, it may be here, at school, in the early years that they learn diligence and exactitude, so obviously the hallmark of the Japanese temperament. Be that as it may, one thing is sure, diligence and intelligence are required, and Koshi possessed both. He was a good student and became an expert in the art of brush writing. Evidence of this is to be seen in many a Salvationist's home today, where Hasegawa's texts in artistic, flowing characters have pride of place.

After finishing primary education Koshi spent four years at secondary school. Primary was free, but secondary education had to be paid for, and at this time his parents found difficulty in meeting the increasing expenses of a large, growing family. It so happened that at a time when Koshi's school fee was due on a stipulated date, the money was not forthcoming. This brought great embarrassment to the proud, sensitive boy. He wondered how money could be procured and in his dreams fancied himself among the mailed riders on white horses in Manchuria, of whom he had read, robbing money from the rich to give to the poor!

Meanwhile he applied himself to his studies and his scholastic aptitude won him a place at high school. He enjoyed the teaching there, but the three hours' walk from home to the new school, which was situated in Kobe, and three hours' walk at the end of a strenuous day were rather wearing. It meant leaving home long before sunrise and returning after dark during the cold winter months six days a week, for then, as now, Saturday was a school day in Japan.

Kobe was the nearest big town from Koshi's home. Up

to 1867 it had been a small fishing village, clustered round a sacred Shinto shrine from which came its name, originally Kamibe, meaning 'Keepers of the gods'. Lying sheltered by a range of hills, its natural water-line made an excellent harbour. When Japan shed the isolationist policy and opened its ports to foreign trade, Kobe rapidly developed into the country's largest port.

Koshi often went down to the harbour to watch the great ocean liners arrive. He was fascinated by the many different countries represented and conjured in his mind pictures of the foreign places he had read about and his heart filled with a great longing to see these for himself. He decided that, after graduating from high school, he would train to become a naval officer.

On a sunny September day in 1917, after school examinations were passed with high credit, Koshi left his sheltered life and embarked on his first great adventure. He arrived in Tokyo with few belongings but with lofty ambitions. At first the great city seemed bewildering to the inexperienced youth, the vast network of endless streets, the helter-skelter traffic of trams, rickshaws and other vehicles. He was impressed by the many-storeyed, ornate buildings: the Diet with its imposing central tower, the numerous shrines and temples and, most of all, the Imperial Palace, where the Emperor lived in isolated splendour in the very centre of the concrete city on an emerald green island, spacious and beautiful, surrounded by a medieval moat.

Arrangements had been made for him to stay with an uncle and aunt during the four years of study at the Tokyo Koto Shyosen Gakko, the Tokyo Naval College, at Sukishima, Ettyujima. Hasegawa was determined to do well, yet when it came to the first, stiff examination he was not without fear of failing. His uncle tried to cheer him, offering him a job as carpenter in his own firm if Koshi failed the examination. But he did not fail. He passed with such excellent results that he earned a scholarship for the rest of the course.

These four years at college were the most formative for Hasegawa's life and character. New influences, new impressions, emotions never known before welled up within him. New ideas that were strange to him claimed his attention. Up to then he had never been in close contact with Christianity. His personal religious life was more or less non-existent. While living at home he had gone to the Shinto shrine on special feast days and the Buddhist temple on more solemn occasions, always in a most perfunctory way, his heart had never been involved. Now his elder sister, living in Tokyo, wanted to introduce him to the Christian faith.

It is necessary that I digress here to try and give the reader some little idea of the history of Christianity in Japan. It is a tragic yet glorious story of great courage, deep devotion and patient endurance spanning the centuries.

Francis Xavier, the Jesuit missionary, introduced Christianity into Japan in the year 1549. He came in the wake of Portuguese mariners, the first Europeans to trade with Japan. A sad fact learnt from history is that the gospel of peace and the use of firearms were gifts from Europe introduced simultaneously.

Francis Xavier stayed only two years in Japan, then other priests followed and their missionary endeavours met with considerable success. Many of the feudal lords in the western part of the country and the southern island of Kyushu embraced Christianity. It has been estimated there were some 150,000 converts around the year 1580, and in the early seventeenth century that number was about doubled. Other records put the number of communicants as high as 600,000. Numerical strength may be of minor importance, but the power of their Christian influence was beyond their number. C. R. Boxer writes:

' It would be difficult, if not impossible, to find another highly civilized pagan country where Christianity had made such a mark, not merely in numbers but in influence.'

Alas, these promising beginnings ended in expulsion of missionaries and ruthless persecution.

In the sixteenth century a Portuguese sea-captain told the current ruler, Hideyoshi, that the King of Portugal would begin by sending priests, wait until they had effected conversions and then send armies which, with the aid of the converts, would take over the country. Hideyoshi, recalling that similar events had taken place elsewhere, issued an edict commanding all foreign religious teachers, on pain of death, to depart from Japan within twenty days. Many Christians were crucified and thousands died from torture and privation. It was common practice to order suspected Christians to tread upon the cross or other sacred symbol, and to kill those who refused to comply.

Christianity would have been wiped out, were it not for a handful of Christians who went into hiding but remained faithful to Christ, handing down His teaching from generation to generation, even to this very day.

It was at this time, in 1637, that the Empire of Japan closed all doors to the outside world. For the next two centuries no foreigner could land on Japan's shores and a decree went out instructing that ' no Japanese ship, or boat whatever, nor any native of Japan, shall presume to go out of the country; who acts contrary to this shall die and the ship, with the crew and goods aboard, shall be sequestrated till further order '.

In the annals of history can a more thrilling and heart-stirring story be told than that of the ' hidden Christians ' of Japan? For more than 200 years they kept the flickering candle of faith burning, passing it on to their children and children's children. When, in 1865, a French missionary opened a new church in Nagasaki, in Kyushu, a small group of men, women and children came up to him and one whispered in his ear: ' The heart of all of us is the same as yours.' Today a national monument stands at this place to mark the event.

As already mentioned, Commodore Perry's arrival shattered Japan's seclusion and motivated many changes. In 1858 the American Consul-general, Townsend Harris, negotiated a treaty for freedom of worship and the establishment of chapels and cemeteries for foreigners. A cessation of anti-Christian persecution was declared in 1873, and in 1889 a law granting freedom to worship according to the Christian religion was enacted. Official recognition of Christianity, as one of Japan's three major religions, came in February 1912 through a Government sponsored ' Conference of Three Religions ' held in Tokyo. Translation of the New Testament had been published in 1880, followed by the Old Testament in 1888.

In that year, too, a young Japanese lad of sixteen knelt on the floor between shelves of Monotype in a printing office and with head bent low prayed: ' O God, I am only a weak, insufficient and unworthy servant of Thine. But, as I offer my body, soul and all to Thee, wilt Thou not accept me and cleanse me? And wilt Thou use and lead me to work for the salvation of the common people, to be a man who conveys the message of the gospel in a language to be understood by the uneducated, one who writes the truth in the way that anyone can read it and be enlightened? I ask this in the name of Jesus, Amen.'

This was Gunpei Yamamuro. Only a year earlier he had embraced Christianity and, in his spare time, now preached the gospel together with other young men of the Gospel Society, although more often he stood alone, witnessing for Christ to the great crowds visiting the temples and shrines. He was mocked and sometimes stoned or knocked down, but he continued his street evangelism. He also had great concern for the souls of his fellow-employees and invited them to Christian meetings. When they refused the invitation, saying they could not understand what was being said or read from the Bible, Gunpei felt keenly that he should make every effort to find some way to rectify this; hence his earnest prayer that God would work through him for the salvation of the common people. And God did use him. In spite of lack of money and influence, he gained entrance to the Christian University of Doshisha in Kyoto.

During student days he was asked to accompany one of his college friends on a visit to Mr. Ishii, then sick in hospital. A keen Christian, a social worker and head of an orphanage, Mr. Ishii had received an English book he was eager to read. Unable to understand it, he had sent for his young university friends. The book was William Booth's *In Darkest England and the Way Out*, and its immediate effect on Yamamuro was to strengthen his desire to serve the common people.

After graduation he became an assistant pastor. Finding he was not given enough opportunity to minister among the people for whom he had a special calling, he turned to other occupations. For a while he worked as a barber, speaking to his customers of spiritual things and all that matters most in life. Then he turned to farming, and later the building trade, sharing the gospel with carpenters and bricklayers.

At this point, in 1895, his friend Mr. Ishii heard of the arrival of The Salvation Army in Japan. He asked Yamamuro to meet the missionaries and take a letter of introduction he had received from an English evangelist. Yamamuro, on greeting these earnest Christians, not only asked questions on behalf of Mr. Ishii, but also found answers to many of his own searchings. Given a copy of *Orders and Regulations for Soldiers*, which he studied carefully, he was greatly impressed by the practical application of Christianity to the everyday life of ordinary people. Here was the expression of religion for which he had been looking. He felt he had found what his fellow countrymen needed. When discussing it with Mr. Ishii, the elder man said to Yamamuro: ' You have found the key to your life's service.'

After attending Salvation Army meetings for two months Yamamuro became the first Japanese Salvation Army officer. And this was the man whom Suga San, Koshi's elder sister, desired her brother to hear.

*Chapter
Three*

FROM NAVY TO ARMY

SUGA SAN, twelve years senior to Koshi, had journeyed to Tokyo to study at the Ochanomizu Women's University while her young brother was still at primary school in Kobe. During this period, a relative of Mrs. Yamamuro came to the college to lecture on the Christian faith. Drawn immediately to those noble ideals and high standards, Suga San began attending Salvation Army meetings at Kanda, not far from her college. Here she heard Gunpei Yamamuro clearly and concisely expounding the tenets of Christianity.

As she listened she drew comparisons between her own religion and this, to her, new faith. She recognized certain similarities. Christ, like Buddha, came with a message of peace. Christian principles resembled the Buddhist system of ethics in its conception of love and compassion to all men. She was well acquainted with the idea of self-denial as also taught in the Four Noble Truths. The demand for daily discipline in thought, word and deed was ever before her as a Buddhist; but the fact that she never attained her ideal was a constant cause for regret. Her own conception of an Ultimate Reality was vague and uncertain. Now she heard that God is love, and that He had sent His Son to be the means by which our sins are forgiven; that Jesus Christ took upon Himself our sin and guilt on the Cross; and that the Holy Spirit gives power to live a good life. No longer would she have to strive toward perfection in her own strength; not through her own good deeds could salvation be attained, it was the gift of God received by faith.

As she listened to Gunpei Yamamuro speaking, a feeling of great awe came over her and an awareness of God's presence was born in her innermost being. She felt moved to kneel in complete self-surrender, asking Him to guide her through life.

From the first contact Suga San had had with Salvationists she had been attracted by their positive religious faith. They had a certainty about their beliefs which appealed to her; she found their fervour infectious. As she contemplated becoming a member or, as they termed it, soldier of Christ in The Salvation Army, she wanted to know more about this 'Army' which, in some aspects, seemed different from other Christian churches. She discovered it was a world-wide organization concerned with the total redemption of man, following their Master's example of combining preaching the gospel with compassionate service.

Its Founder, William Booth, on visiting Japan in 1907, had captivated the imagination of his hearers by his powerful message and his visit was still spoken of by many. Through this man's vision a party of fourteen officers of different nationalities had, in 1895, been sent to commence the work of The Salvation Army in Japan.

Of the many Japanese who had joined the Salvationist ranks a number were women. Suga San was intrigued to see them actively taking part in public work. She realized that personal conviction and devotion to a cause must have overcome their inherent shyness.

Among them was Mrs. Yamamuro whom she greatly admired. Of noble birth, belonging to an old Samurai family, Mrs. Yamamuro had dedicated her life to the uplift of fallen women, caring for them in a rescue home, raising funds for their upkeep. Gentle and refined, she shed around her an influence of purity and light. By nature reticent, her religious conviction compelled her to front-line action, and with her husband and other

FROM NAVY TO ARMY

Salvationists she marched the streets of Tokyo proclaiming the gospel of Christ, and with them she took her place at the rostrum expounding the word of God.

Before long Suga San became a Salvation Army soldier and, relinquishing her post as teacher, entered the now well-established Salvation Army training college. After completing training, she was commissioned Probationary-Lieutenant and appointed to the Young People's Department at Territorial Headquarters, where, among other duties, she did secretarial work for Gunpei Yamamuro.

When Koshi came to Tokyo to study at the Naval College his elder sister wanted to share her faith in a living God with her young brother. Frequently he called in to see her at the office where she was working, and while he enjoyed the tea she made him and munched the bun he had brought himself, she talked enthusiastically about her work, her joy in the Lord Jesus Christ and her admiration for Yamamuro San, especially his wonderful interpretation of the Bible.

Koshi's interest was stirred. He decided to hear the man for himself. So he began to attend Salvation Army meetings at Kanda Hall, attached to Headquarters. Sitting up on the balcony in his trim, black uniform, the young student listened with rapt attention as Yamamuro spoke. He was amazed that this earnest, highly intelligent person could speak so simply about great and profound truths. It made a deep impression on him, and as he listened week by week Koshi felt that here was a religion demanding a conduct equal to its claims. He deplored the lack of any absolute standards in the world he knew; he was dissatisfied with himself, realizing he was just drifting without any definite aim or purpose in life. Often he was troubled with questions that came to his mind and which he could not answer, yet they clamoured for attention. Was there any meaning to life? What happened after death? Who could tell him? Where could he find an answer? He needed someone to guide him, so that his life would have purpose; an ideal to help him strive toward high and noble living.

His sister had given him a copy of *The Common People's Gospel*, a translation of stories from the Gospels into colloquial Japanese with illustrations drawn from everyday life, written by Gunpei Yamamuro. He began to read it with great interest. As he turned its pages he understood that here, in the person of Jesus Christ, was the Ideal, the Guide he was seeking.

One evening at Kanda Hall, Yamamuro spoke on the atonement of Christ. His words came with conviction, strong and simple: ' Christ died for our sins. To reconcile sinful man with his Maker, Christ shed His Blood on the Cross. God came down to man in human form to lift man up to life with Him. God shows His love for us in that while we were yet sinners Christ died for us. God, in Christ, bore the penalty of our sin. The Cross is God's victory over evil, sin and death.'

When he concluded with the words, ' Love, so amazing, so divine, demands your life, your soul, your all ', Hasegawa was under deep conviction. Feeling great indebtedness to Christ, and with the inborn sense of moral obligation of repayment which is an integral part of the Japanese rule of life, he knew he would have to act. Christ had given His life for him; he could not ignore so noble a deed.

When Yamamuro, at the close of the meeting, pointed to the gallery, where Hasegawa was sitting on the front row, and said, ' You, too, must accept Christ as your Saviour,' Koshi felt sure it was a personal invitation to him. He rose to his feet and came down from the gallery, walking with determined tread down the aisle, and knelt at the Penitent-form giving himself to the Christ who had given Himself for him. Often during later life, when referring to his conversion, Hasegawa would say: ' It was the love of Christ that won me.'

On completion of four years' training at the Naval College, Koshi Hasegawa was appointed Naval Reserve Officer. It was a proud day for the young man, marking the first achievement of his ambition. All eyes were on the fine youth receiving his commission, taller than most of his comrades, erect in bearing and looking every inch an officer. Full of promise, life lay before him. Adventure was beckoning. His childhood dream to visit far distant countries could now be fulfilled. The ship, to which he was appointed, embarked on a global voyage.

Little is known about this period in Hasegawa's life except that combining high standards of Christian living with sea adventures, especially for one new to the Christian faith, could not have been easy. From the commencement of his naval career Hasegawa determined to make known to all that as a Christian he could never take part in anything out of harmony with Christian principles. In all probability he was the only Christian on the ship; to the other seafaring men a believer in a strange and foreign religion. But Hasegawa's faith was firmly grounded in Christ. He spent much of his leisure studying the Bible and in lonely vigils, with only the sky and the sea around him, his soul drew strength from the Eternal God.

He had a great love of music and his violin was his constant companion; to play it gave him immense pleasure. What solace to the soul to take up an instrument and pour out one's innermost longings; or to strum out one's frustrations and failures and feel cleansed and renewed! So we see this young, sensitive naval officer taking his violin up on deck, matching his playing to the mood of the sea; the stars looking down on the speck of a ship on the vast ocean, and Hasegawa pouring out his soul in music.

While the ship was on the high seas a sailor fell overboard. The captain showed no concern. The vessel, due in harbour by a certain time was, according to schedule, already late. 'No time to stop and commence rescue operation; the fellow's just an ordinary sailor, of no importance to anyone,' said the captain. Hasegawa thought differently. With courage he faced the captain and persuaded him to let down a lifeboat. The sailor's life was saved. Possessed of an inner strength which his outward, gentle appearance and manners belied, Hasegawa, always softly spoken, quiet and reticent, exerted an iron will when it came to matters of principle. This he exercised right through life.

On the ship's return to Japan after a year abroad, Hasegawa's health showed signs of trouble. He became seriously ill. It was discovered that his lungs were affected. To his great disappointment his career in the Navy had to be temporarily broken. Complete rest was essential. One of his brothers living in Kobe invited him to share his home, and gradually Koshi's health was restored. This experience was to Hasegawa like that of the Apostle Paul waiting in the desert of Arabia, taken away from the stream of life, tarrying, alone with God, biding His time to show the way and direct his footsteps.

When he had fully regained health, Hasegawa reported for duty at Naval Headquarters and was told to take up a post on land in Tokyo. This never materialized. The year was 1923, the year of the great Kanto earthquake that rocked the south-eastern part of Honshu, destroyed half of Tokyo and left neighbouring Yokohama a heap of rubble.

With sickening heart Hasegawa heard of the happenings in Tokyo; 316,000 buildings had been destroyed or damaged, among them the Salvation Army Territorial Headquarters and the Kanda Corps hall, where he had first heard the salvation message and knelt at the Penitent-form giving himself to Christ. With great sorrow he learnt that one of the officers, the editor of *The War Cry*, Brigadier Kazuo Sashida, had been crushed to death

FROM NAVY TO ARMY

beneath debris as the building collapsed. His own sister, Suga, no longer working at Headquarters, had been transferred two years previously to the U.S.A. and had married Captain Soichi Ozaki, a Japanese officer serving in America.

Life in Tokyo was completely disrupted by the earthquake and Hasegawa's appointment changed. He was posted to the small island of Okinajima, in the Japan Sea, to teach at the nautical school. This he accepted as the next step in God's plan for his life.

During the waiting period while ill, a desire to serve God more effectually had been born within him. Here on this island, where he was now living, the number of Christians was small. Here he witnessed to the Christian faith and tried to bring others into God's Kingdom. He started by inviting a few people to his room, where he read the Bible and explained the text in simple language, then told of his own conversion. As he gained courage he started preaching in the streets, carrying with him the Army flag of yellow, red and blue. This created a considerable stir, both of curiosity and consternation: a Japanese naval officer following a 'foreign' flag in the midst of a people to whom the emblem of the 'rising sun on the white field' is sacrosanct. He was the sole Salvationist on the island. The nearest corps was Yonago, on the mainland, where he was registered as a soldier and where he attended whenever he had occasion to leave the island. He never failed to send a tenth of his income every month to the corps to further God's work.

Thus it went on for some time. More people attended the Bible classes, some became Christians; but the head of the school was not pleased. One day Hasegawa was called to his office and told that Christian propaganda must stop. But Hasegawa, with courage similar to that of Peter and John when commanded by Jewish authority to stop speaking of the risen Christ, told the head of the school that he had to speak of the things God had done for him; God was his highest authority. It was left to the head to decide whether he would let Hasegawa carry on with his single-handed evangelism or lose one of his best teachers in the school. As he was not prepared for the latter, he cautioned Hasegawa at least to keep his meetings quiet.

These days of solitary witnessing bore fruit. Many years later an officer appointed to Hokkaido, the most northern island in the Japan archipelago, was, on arrival at his destination, met by the wife of the town mayor. She, whose father had been the chief of Okinajima island, had been led to Christ through Hasegawa's testimony when he taught at the nautical school. Remaining faithful to the Christian faith, she had for years given full support to the Salvation Army corps in the town where she now lived. 'Cast thy bread upon the waters: for thou shalt find it after many days.'

News of Hasegawa's staunch Salvationism, flying the Army flag single-handed in Okinajima, reached Headquarters in Tokyo, and Colonel Yamamuro decided to visit the island when next touring in that part of the country. Yamamuro's name was by this time well known throughout the country as an outstanding scholar and author of many books. Before arriving on the island, he received an invitation to give a lecture on The Salvation Army to the students of the nautical school.

After the lecture Hasegawa and some of the students invited the Colonel for a boat trip round the island. Yamamuro graciously accepted. Hasegawa went ahead of the others to see that the boat was in ship-shape order and all was ready for the trip. Slippers were put out in readiness for the passengers. As Colonel Yamamuro was about to step aboard Hasegawa said politely, 'The sailor loves his boat as if it were his home, so would you mind taking off your shoes and putting on these slippers?'

FROM NAVY TO ARMY

Yamamuro smilingly consented and slipped into the offered slippers, for he, too, was Japanese and understood. Through his action the students' respect for their teacher deepened and they regarded this Christian preacher from Tokyo with a new and higher esteem both for having shown respect for their boat and for his Christian humility.

It was December 31, 1928, the night which changed the whole course of Hasegawa's life. New Year's Eve, celebrated by all, is a time when families gather together. Hasegawa's thoughts went to his childhood home. For him there were no celebrations; he was standing in for another teacher and therefore on duty at the school. Around him all was quiet. Only the steady lapping of the waves against the rocks broke the stillness of the night. Distant bells began to ring out the one hundred and eight sins of the world, offering a new beginning for the year 1929.

Hasegawa opened his Bible, his eyes alighting on the words of Jesus to Simon Peter: ' Simon son of John, do you love Me more than all else? '

In the stillness of the midnight hour Christ's voice spoke. Instead of ' Simon son of John ', it was ' Hasegawa Koshi, do you love Me more than all else? More than your boat? More than your naval career? More than your life? If so, feed My lambs.'

He sat deep in thought for a long time. Christ had spoken; of that he was sure. He had called him to leave his post, to offer himself for full-time service in The Salvation Army. How could he? At twenty-eight years of age he was older than the stipulated limit for candidateship. Other considerations weighed against his becoming a Salvation Army officer. Although he had recovered from his illness, the scar would always remain on his lungs; he could never expect to enjoy robust health. Yet the words, so clear at the midnight hour, kept ringing in his ears:

' Hasegawa Koshi, do you love Me more than all else? '
Yes, he loved his Lord and Master, and was willing to give up all and go to the ends of the earth for Him.

The arrival of an encouraging letter from Colonel Yamamuro Hasegawa took as a further sign that God could use him as an officer in The Salvation Army. When the New Year holidays were over he wrote to the Commanding Officer of Yonago Corps for candidate forms and, in faith, sent his resignation to Naval Headquarters requesting that he be released from the Navy.

In August 1929 Hasegawa, having been honourably discharged from the Navy, entered the Salvation Army Training College in Tokyo. He was once again a cadet—not in the Navy but in the ' Save-the-world Army '.

*Chapter
Four*

CHO THE BUTTERFLY

AT the beginning of the twentieth century a Japanese family, by the name of Saito, made the long journey from the most southern island of Kyushu to Manchuria in the north. The part of Manchuria to which they were going had recently been ceded to Japan by Russia, who had earlier leased it from China. It was bordering on Russia to the north, Inner Mongolia to the west and Korea to the south.

Saito San, son of the secretary to the island's ruler, was a building contractor and saw possibilities to expand his trade in this still undeveloped and remote area and to make a good living for his growing family.

Little Cho, the eldest daughter, had just turned nine when the family made their journey north. She was a sprightly child who could never sit still. Her name, meaning ' butterfly ', was most appropriate. She would dart from one task to another with boundless energy and dexterity, as a butterfly flits from flower to flower. She was not, by common standards, a pretty child, but any lack of generally accepted ' good looks ' was amply redeemed by her vivacity and zest for life.

Six sons and another daughter completed the Saito family. Saito-Okusan (Mrs. Saito) must often have blessed her eldest daughter for her energy and willingness to help bring up her younger brothers and sister. It is common knowledge, and quite the accepted thing in Japan, that the male section of the community is spoiled by the so-called ' weaker sex '. Boys early discover that they are specially privileged beings, as mothers and sisters quite happily wait on them and, as far as possible, grant their every wish. Not so in the Saito family! Cho, being the eldest, exerted her particular rights and saw that the younger brothers took their share in the household chores, and because of her ever cheerful spirit, they looked up to her with respect and affection.

As with most families living away from customary environment, the Saitos tried to make their home a part of the ' old country '; the house which father built was typically Japanese. The outside walls were unpainted wood for, according to Japanese belief, wood must be left free to breathe. The rooms were divided by sliding doors of thin wooden frames covered with fragile rice paper, which had to be replaced whenever a child had the misfortune to poke a finger through, though this was surprisingly infrequent. Some rooms had *tatami* floors, layers of straw-matting making a resilient base for sleeping and saving space that beds would otherwise take up. Ample provision for storing bedding during the day was found in spacious wall cupboards. In the living room was the traditional *tokonoma*, an elevated alcove in which objects of art and beauty—a hanging scroll, a flower arrangement are displayed. To make the house snug and warm during the long, cold winter months, a Russian oven, called *pechica*, was filled with coal every morning. The house, like most Japanese houses, had little protection from intruders, a fact which strikes most overseas visitors to Japan. One wonders whether easy access to each other's possessions has something to do with their sense of honesty; possessions being equally assailable, was honesty found to be the best policy? It depends, of course, whether environment makes the man, or man the environment.

In the Saito household the old traditions of Buddhism and Shintoism were practised regularly and the whole rigid pattern of behaviour in Japanese family life of those days was strictly adhered to. Father's authority was

Koshi Hasegawa — the youngest among his brothers

At the time of marriage

As
Training Principal

With his 1969
motto: 'The Ye
of Soul-Saving'

unquestioned; but it was not considered irksome, for the Saito children loved and respected their father, who was an upright and good-living man, even though he liked his *sake* (Japanese rice liquor).

In the home could be seen both Buddhist and Shinto shrines similar to those found in most Japanese homes. Once a month Obo San, the Buddhist priest, came to read lessons on the ' Four Noble Truths ' and the ' Noble Eightfold Path '. The language used in the ' Holy Books ' read by Obo San was completely unintelligible to the children and they always tried to disappear when they saw him coming, but they never succeeded! The parents ensured that all the children were present, sitting in orderly rows on the floor. If any of them started to fidget, a look from father was enough to bring them into line again.

Occasional visits to the public shrines were happily anticipated by the children for two particular reasons: one was the ride to the shrine in a special cart, elaborately decorated; the other was the delicacies that mother prepared and the sweets to be bought at the booths near the shrine. They were happy events which Cho enjoyed during her childhood because of the carefree holiday atmosphere, but they had no religious significance for her whatsoever.

The O'Bon festival celebrated in mid-July each year brought a spirit of great solemnity into the home. This was the time when the spirits of dead ancestors visited the altar sacred to them in each household. Special offerings of food were prepared and placed before the altar. The children were told of the many virtues of former generations and reminded to follow their example and never to bring dishonour to their name. This sober occasion was brightened by coloured lanterns lit to guide the wandering souls.

The Third of March every year was of special importance for Cho and her younger sister. Just as the boys have their particular day in May, so the girls have theirs in March, called *Hinamatsuri*, the Doll's Festival. It is said that the first *hinamatsuri* was held by the royal family in 1629, and soon copied by members of the noble classes, then later taken up by the ordinary people, till it became a national holiday. Dolls, dressed as king and queen with maids and musicians and other imposing figures of the royal household, are placed on small platforms amid ornamental paper-lamps and peach blossom.

Tradition maintains that even before the *hinamatsuri* was instituted by the royal family, a kind of ceremony had taken place about this time of year. Parents would fashion dolls out of paper and let them sail away in paper boats, praying that any evil spirit that might attack their children's health would sail away with the dolls.

These dolls have disappeared for good, but the dolls of the royal household remain, and fortunate is the girl who possesses a full set. They are often handed down from mother to daughter as treasured heirlooms. A few days before the Third of March Cho and her sister had great fun setting up the dolls for friends and family to admire. There were fifteen dolls in all, each on a stand forming a court scene with the king and queen and royal attendants. Paper screens and miniature ornaments exquisitely worked completed the scene. In those days it was generally believed by girls that the dolls had to be put safely away as soon as the day was over; any delay in so doing would mean delay in marriage. It would seem that Cho must have disregarded this belief, for she had to wait quite a few years before she found her partner in life!

After Cho had finished school she attended a women's college of art. It is important for Japanese women to be well versed in cultured living. She was taught etiquette, the intricate system of good manners belonging to this ancient nation: the manifold 'don'ts' which a cultured lady must observe, such as not to sit with crossed legs when sitting on a chair, not to laugh without covering her mouth with the palm of her hand, to bow low to her superior and those older in years, and not too low to her equals. It must have been irksome for Cho with her freedom-loving ways, and the many restrictions could well have seemed burdensome.

She was taught the ancient tea-ceremony, the *cha-no-yu*, regarded as ' an institution of disciplinary training for the promotion of enlightenment and mental composure '. Originally it was Zen ritual, where the monks gathered before the image of Bodhidharma and drank tea out of a single bowl with the formality of a holy sacrament. It has changed with the years, but is still looked upon as ' a religion of the art of life ' in which one appreciates the artistic atmosphere through the medium of the delicate aroma of powdered tea. The simple setting of the tea room, the elegant beauty of the utensils and the graceful ritual of the ceremony is meant to foster a devotion to simplicity, a love of beauty and a spirit of tranquillity.

Tranquillity of nature was not one of Cho's virtues and the hours-long ceremony bored her, but she revelled in the arts and crafts which she was taught, and her vivid imagination and creative skill found expression through her deft fingers in creating all sorts of articles and objects of beauty. This wonderful skill has been a great asset throughout her life and she has used it to good advantage in teaching other women.

Every well-educated Japanese woman is also taught the complex art of *ikebana*, flower arrangement. To the uninitiated it may seem possible to learn in thirteen easy lessons. Far from it! Even to arrange a single Japanese peony takes hours and hours of lessons and can be done expertly only by those well versed in the art. There are two main divisions in the style followed: the formal and the natural. The Japanese favour the formal. To this belongs the well-known ' heaven-earth-man ' style, where flowers and leaves represent these three in their particular arrangement. Cho excelled at this and won prizes for her original displays.

Most of all she loved her lessons in playing the koto, a horizontal harp or zither made of one piece of wood with thirteen strings resting on a bridge. It is played with a long, slender plectrum held in the right hand. When the strings are stroked with the left hand a melancholy, whining sound is produced, contrasting with the pert, gay sound of plucked strings in staccato movement. The music moves from full notes to quarter and half notes in fanciful revelry, to the enjoyment of performer and listener alike. Even today, fifty years or more later, Cho takes out her koto on special occasions and strokes its strings lovingly.

After graduating from college, Cho took a post as nursery school teacher. She was fond of children and they of her, and they quickly responded to her warm personality and enthusiasm. She liked her work, and yet there seemed something missing in her life; something so intangible that she could not even put it into words—a longing for something unobtainable, an assurance of the purpose of life, a reaching out for something higher than the routine of daily living.

When she took the children under her care to the Buddhist temple on the feast of the birthday of Gautama Buddha, the whole formality suddenly struck her as meaningless and without any real significance. She started thinking about the difference between worship and daily conduct, and here it seemed to her that the one had nothing to do with the other, yet, in her own mind she felt the two ought to agree.

Her parents, aware of her listlessness at this time, mistakenly took it as desire for marriage, for she was well over twenty years of age. Through relatives and friends they started to negotiate for a suitable partner. Photographs

CHO THE BUTTERFLY

of prospective 'candidates' were procured for Cho to choose from. But Cho was not interested. Nevertheless, a young doctor, an acquaintance of the family, applied for her hand. Regarded as a most suitable match, the parents went ahead with preparations, purchasing the expensive wedding kimono and even furniture to set up a new home. But Cho had a stubborn will. She did not feel ready for marriage, neither had she any inclination to share her life with someone she did not know or respect. To her father's great displeasure she refused to fall in with their plans, even though she realized they had her happiness at heart and had done all as they thought for the best.

Round about this time she began to receive letters from the brother next in age to herself, who was studying at the university in Nagasaki, in southern Japan. Tadayuki San had become a Christian and now wanted to share his new-found joy with his elder sister. He wrote regularly and quoted Bible texts in every letter and on every postcard, pointing out the way of salvation and emphasizing God's love in seeking to bring back His lost children to a right relationship with their Heavenly Father.

This was all completely new to Cho. She had never set eyes on a Bible and knew nothing of the Christian religion. But God knew Cho and was seeking her.

Dairen, the port city on Liaotung peninsula, facing the Yellow Sea, was half an hour's walk from Cho's house, and this was where she now was working as a kindergarten teacher.

When part of Manchuria had come under Japanese jurisdiction The Salvation Army had sent Japanese officers to serve the growing Japanese community. A home for mothers and children was opened, housing about one hundred; the gospel was preached; and eventually four corps were established, the largest of which (with 300 soldiers or more) was in Dairen. The name of Annie Smyth is remembered and held in high regard by many

Japanese who lived in Dairen at the time, as well as by ships' officers from all parts of the world. It was through the efforts of this intrepid missionary officer collecting money from the boats in Dairen harbour that the fine, brick building which became the corps 'citadel' was built.

Here, Cho's younger brothers and sister began attending Sunday-school. When passing the hall one Sunday morning, one of the boys had been invited in by the Commanding Officer, Captain Hitotsuyanegi. He had enjoyed the meeting so much that he brought the rest of the younger end of the family, and they now attended regularly every Sunday. When the boy told the Captain about his elder sister who was a teacher, the Captain sent Cho a special invitation to attend a Sunday night meeting.

Cho was not keen on going, but the youngsters kept on pestering her, saying that if she did not come they would stop going. She realized the children had found something they enjoyed and she did not want to take their pleasure away from them, so she wrote and asked her student brother in Nagasaki for his advice. Back came the reply by return of post: 'Please go to The Salvation Army.' She, like her young brothers and sister, enjoyed the bright singing, but she had no idea what the Captain was talking about. She listened intently as he was pleading with 'sinners' to repent. Cho was bewildered. Who was he talking about? Was he talking to her? Why was she a sinner? She had never thought of herself as such. She knew she was not by any means perfect, but then who was? She had always tried to restrain any unworthy impulse. She believed in self-restraint, which to the Japanese is part of self-respect. Now it seemed she was told she was a sinner and needed salvation. She recognized some of the words the Captain used, from the Bible texts her brother had sent her. One was: 'But God commendeth His love toward us, in that, while we were yet sinners, Christ died for us.' She had been wondering a lot about that since first she read it. God loves me—Christ died for me—a sinner. She could not stop thinking about it. She only wished she knew what it really meant and what she was expected to do.

She started attending the early morning prayer meetings held in the hall, before going to the school where she was teaching. After attending every morning for a week, light seemed to penetrate her mind. She began to understand why she was a sinner and needed the gift of salvation. She had ignored God, had not lived in obedience to His will. She had lived her own life, thinking only of herself, her own desires, her own pleasures. Now she began to understand that the whole purpose of life was to love God and live for Him; God had created man for Himself. She began to realize that man's selfishness had created a barrier between God and man and, in order to break down that barrier, Christ had come to earth to mediate between God and man and bring them into a loving relationship.

The thought that Christ should have given His life for her awakened such deep emotions within her that when the Captain asked her one Sunday morning if she would follow Christ, she answered firmly, 'Tonight I will decide to follow Him.' And Cho was true to her words. When the invitation was given in the salvation meeting for anyone to kneel at the Penitent-form and commit themselves to Christ, Cho was the first to come.

So on a bitterly cold night in January 1926, Cho became a Christian. She was then twenty-five years of age. The snow was lying thick on the ground when she walked home. Everything was still; only the crunch of the snow under her feet made a sound in the vast quietness. The stars above her were twinkling with dazzling brightness and within Cho's heart was peace. But she still had to tell her parents that she had become a Christian.

Chapter
Five

THE BUTTERFLY SPREADS HER WINGS

SAITO SAN and Okusan (wife) had not, up to now, opposed their children's interest in the Christian religion, imagining it to be a passing fancy that would keep them amused for a time. But one day when the Buddhist priest came on his usual visit, he saw on the wall a Bible text the younger children had been given in Sunday-school. Annoyed, the Buddhist priest told the parents to remove it and to stop anyone of the family having anything to do with the Christians, or evil spirits would take their revenge.

Cho, in true Japanese tradition, never having questioned her father's authority or wisdom, found it difficult to tell her parents that the Christian religion was now her religion, the Christian's God her God, and even if it displeased her parents she could not now stop attending Salvation Army meetings.

Knowing that Cho frequently attended the Christian place of worship, her parents tried by devious means to keep her away; by arranging outings for the family on Sundays, or making her do certain tasks in the house just before it was time to go to the meeting. Cho would not refuse to do whatever she was asked. She wanted to remain a dutiful daughter, so that her parents could not lay blame on her decision to become a Christian. Completing any set task, with lightning speed, she would run the three kilometres to the hall, arriving late. Sometimes the meeting would even be over; but the Captain, knowing

THE BUTTERFLY SPREADS HER WINGS 53

the fight his convert was putting up for her new faith, would pray with her, read the Bible, speak words of encouragement, then send her home reaffirmed in love for God and determined to be faithful and endure. She kept this up for eight months.

One night the following August, eight months after Cho's conversion, while the evenings were still light, the air warm and sultry, Saito San, Cho's father, had been to town and, together with friends, imbibed too much *sake*. Slightly intoxicated, he decided to confront the Salvation Army people, who to his way of thinking had bewitched his daughter. He had heard rumours that she was going from door to door selling Salvation Army newspapers and it filled him with anger. He had also heard that she stood with others of these misguided people on the streetcorners singing and shouting; she had even been seen carrying a red paper lantern.

' Disgrace! Utter disgrace! ' he muttered to himself, as he approached the Salvation Army hall.

He found the door open—but the hall empty. Entering, he sat down on one of the wooden benches near the big iron stove; not that he chose to sit there for warmth, for the stove was cold on the warm summer's night, but it gave him some kind of shelter. He felt uneasy in these unfamiliar surroundings. Nevertheless, he was determined to wait until someone came who would take him to the person responsible for making such a fool of his daughter.

Half an hour or so went by. He had begun to sober up when he heard a commotion at the door. Turning round he saw the Salvation Army people marching in—his daughter among them carrying the red lantern. He felt distinctly embarrassed and began to wish he had not come, but there was no way of escaping now. His daughter had caught sight of him and it seemed strange that she looked pleased to see him. She touched the arm of one of the more distinguished-looking persons near to her, said something, and together they came toward him with beaming faces.

Cho introduced the person as her Commanding Officer, Captain Hitotsuyanegi—the very person he had come to rebuke. But seeing his mild, kindly face and hearing him say how pleased he was to welcome him to the meeting, Saito San preferred to forget the reason why he had come. Somehow, the angry thoughts that had filled his mind before, did not suit these surroundings. He sat back, intending to find out why everybody seemed so happy. He liked the singing. He watched his daughter out of the corner of his eye. She seemed to sing the loudest, and every time she looked toward him she smiled happily. What was it that had changed her so? What had given her a new zest for life, just when they had thought she was pining for marriage?

When, later in the meeting, he saw different men and women stand to their feet and heard them say, with such great assurance and obvious joy, what it meant to them to have accepted Christ as their Saviour and Lord, he was amazed. Was such a change really possible? Could happiness like that be found? Could it happen to him, although by now the best part of his life was spent? He decided it was worth trying and when the invitation was given for anyone to accept Christ, he made his way to kneel at the front bench. He did not know what to say, he had never knelt like that before, and the Captain had to explain to him what to do. All he knew was that he too wanted the joy and peace of heart he had heard about, and which so obviously had been given to his daughter since she had become a Christian.

Saito San found the joy and peace for which he had sought. He became a new man, eager to wear Salvation Army uniform so that he could witness for God. But first he needed instruction in Christian faith and doctrine. He gave generously to support the work and, so as not to let

THE BUTTERFLY SPREADS HER WINGS

his daughter outshine him, he attended regularly the open-air meetings and even carried the red lantern! He had three new ones made, one of them extra big, which he carried himself, for as he said: ' I must carry this for my Lord; for the Cross He carried for me was heavier than this.' On each of the lanterns was inscribed ' God is Love.' To go out preaching and singing on street corners in this hostile climate, during the winter months, when the snow lay thick on the ground and the icy wind cut through the clothes, called for stamina and strong conviction. Boots would freeze to the ground if their wearer stood too long in one position, but neither Saito San nor Cho would want to miss any opportunity to share their joy with others, for there were many who had never heard about Christ.

Three months after Saito San's conversion a cottage meeting was held in their home. The Captain and his wife and Salvationists came from Dairen. Saito San had invited friends and neighbours. In this meeting Cho's mother was converted and now the whole family shared a wonderful Christian fellowship.

The night of Cho's conversion she had noticed the words ' God needs you ' hanging on the wall in the hall. They attracted her attention every time she went in. They seemed to have special meaning. She spent hours thinking about them. Could it be that God needed her for some special work? She was content with her present life; her work among the children in the kindergarten gave her a great deal of satisfaction. In her spare time she was always busy in the corps, and had had the joy of seeing many young people converted. But the words ' God needs you ' would not leave her. She could see them written before her even when she closed her eyes and could hear them whispered from the depth of her inner consciousness. She wanted to give God her whole life and to serve Him wherever He thought best.

Cho spoke to her parents about the possibility of becoming a Salvation Army officer and dedicating herself to God in the Army. This would mean going to the training college in Tokyo, a long way to travel for a young single woman. The parents tried to persuade her against it. Were there not enough people in Manchuria who did not know the true God? Why need she go to Tokyo? Could she not do just as good a work here? Could she not take up some special responsibility in the corps as a local officer? God would surely honour the work she did for Him here. The thought of their young daughter leaving them and her sheltered home life to go out into the unknown, filled them with apprehension. Surely God would not demand that.

So Cho stayed at home. But she could not suppress the silent whisper within her heart however much she engaged in work in the corps. Neither did she feel at this time that she could go against her parents' wish.

Two years later Saito San became seriously ill and was admitted to hospital. He had cancer and there was little hope for his recovery.

One Sunday in May, Captain and Mrs. Hitotsuyanegi with some of the soldiers from the corps, including Cho, came to hold a meeting in the hospital ward in which Saito San was lying. When the meeting was over and the others had gone, Cho remained alone with her father. Saito San found it difficult to speak, but he took his daughter's hand and whispered: 'We didn't want you to become an officer, to leave home. This was because of our human feelings. But God has spoken to me and said, "What you cannot do I, God, can do," so I offer you now to God.'

He sank back on the pillow, a smile full of peace lit up his face, and with this his spirit left its earthen vessel. God had taken him to Himself.

In August 1928 Cho said good-bye to her mother, her

THE BUTTERFLY SPREADS HER WINGS

younger sister and brothers, and set out alone on the long journey from Manchuria to Tokyo. She was in high spirits; her great desire to become a Salvation Army officer was soon to be fulfilled. Life to her was a great adventure. She was overjoyed at the prospect of seeing the great city of Tokyo and other places of which she had heard so much during her childhood, but as the train sped through the Japanese countryside she was overcome by a feeling of loneliness. She looked out of the window at the passing scene; this was not quite what she had expected, the general scenery was one of drabness. Poverty showed its ugly head in many forms, in the shabbiness of the buildings and the dull look of people's clothing.

It was not long before she realized that she herself, as a Salvation Army officer, had to accept poverty as her own way of life, although never drab poverty. No longer could she call a rickshaw and be carried by someone else; she now had to use her own two legs wherever she wanted to go.

Cadet Cho entered into college life with her customary verve and zest. She was quick and receptive in classes; she had much to learn and some things to unlearn. She studied Salvation Army doctrine and Orders and Regulations assiduously; but her happiest days were when she was out on corps work mingling with the people, talking to the children on the streets, visiting from door to door.

The year went by quickly and soon she was to take up her first appointment as a fully fledged Salvation Army officer. The day of Commissioning arrived. The Central Hall at Kanda was filled with friends and relatives of the cadets, all eager to know where the young people were to be sent. The young officers in their new uniforms lined the platform, looking rather tense with repressed emotion. Cho's name was called. She stepped out in front of the Territorial Commander and saluted. Then she heard the order: ' Probationary-Lieutenant Saito Cho—you are appointed to assist at Kibōkan—Osaka Women's Home.'

* * * *

For centuries a system of licensed prostitution had existed in Japan. Girls could be openly sold for a fixed period. Then, in 1872, an Imperial Ordinance abolished this practice and ordered the release of all licensed prostitutes. Unfortunately, this did not lead to reform, for the people who were making money from the nefarious trade knew how to dodge the law. Sometimes because of poverty, parents would part with a daughter, and sometimes because of vicious avarice, girls were 'loaned' for a sum of money to the brothel-houses, like goods in a pawnbroker's hand. The girls would have to agree to be licensed prostitutes in the house of the keeper until the loan was repaid. Police regulation prevented any girl from leaving a licensed house without the signature of the brothel-keeper. If she tried to escape she would invariably be caught by the police, punished and sent back to the brothel.

An American Methodist missionary, U. G. Murphy, obtained a judicial ruling that a person could not be deprived of liberty on account of debt. He also drew attention to the Japanese law prohibiting the purchase and sale of human beings. The rule which had bound prostitutes must therefore be considered null and void. Still no change was brought about in the girls' sordid plight. The police simply refused to carry out the court's order.

At the turn of the century Commissioner Henry Bullard, then Territorial Commander of Japan, together with Japanese officers, Yamamuro Gunpei and his wife Kiye in the forefront, decided to fight openly this social evil. A special rescue number of the *Toki-no-Koe* (*The War Cry*) was issued. On its front page, in bold characters, was printed the operative clause of the 1872 Imperial Ordinance, in language that even the lesser educated could understand. Together with this was a declaration

THE BUTTERFLY SPREADS HER WINGS

of The Salvation Army's intention to protect and aid all who wished to leave licensed quarters.

About fifty officers spent a whole night in prayer seeking courage and divine guidance for the difficult and dangerous task on which they had embarked. The following day two parties marched behind the Army flag into the most notorious quarter, Yoshawara, in Tokyo, distributing the papers, offering freedom and protection.

They were met with violent opposition from the brothel keepers who regarded it as an assault on their livelihood. They set upon the Salvation Army officers and hammered them mercilessly; many were badly injured. But through this encounter, facing the evil-doers in their den, the interest of the public was aroused. Newspapers sided with The Salvation Army and demanded that girls should be free to leave the brothels if they so desired. The dormant conscience of the people was aroused and came to life. It became a national concern. Some were anxious about the image Japan was presenting abroad. Government could do nothing but respond to the nation-wide agitation. On October 2, 1900 an ordinance was signed by the Emperor declaring that the name of any girl who wanted to be freed, and stated so at a police-station, must be at once removed from the register irrespective of any ' indebtedness ' to the keepers of the house concerned. Anyone not observing this rule would be liable to severe punishment.

No less than 12,000 young women obtained their freedom during the first year the new ordinance was in operation. Many of them were homeless and had nowhere to go. The Salvation Army opened rescue homes and Yamamuro's wife, Kiye, was the first to establish one such home in Tokyo, where she personally cared for and looked after newly released girls, showing them through Christian love a better way of life. Other homes were opened in the provinces. To such a home in the city of

Osaka Lieutenant Saito Cho was appointed after her days of training in Tokyo.

It was not the kind of work she would have chosen. She had hoped to be sent to a corps appointment. She loved being out among the people, but here she felt cooped-up day and night with the same, rather disagreeable women. Her restless spirit and boundless energy had not enough outlet within the confines of an institution. She was young, like most of the women she had been sent to help, but felt no affinity with them, thinking them ill-mannered and quarrelsome. Often they tried her patience. Much of her time was taken up with mundane duties which she felt a servant could just as well be employed to do. She had visualized herself as a preacher of the gospel seeing men and women changed; here she saw no results for her labour. It was just a daily grind. Yet she knew God had called her to become an officer in The Salvation Army and she had accepted her appointment as God's will for her life.

After a trying day with much quarrelling among the women of the home, Cho sat in her room alone, a load of disappointment weighing her down. Was there any point in continuing in this way? She just wasn't getting through to the women whom she wanted to help. There seemed to be a barrier between them and herself. Was it pride that held her back? Was she lacking in compassion?

As she sat thinking these thoughts, suddenly she was startled by the sound of screaming. It was a woman's voice and came from outside the house. Cho rushed out and ran in the direction of the voice. She reached the well. One of the women, a young girl still in her teens, had tried to commit suicide by jumping into the well. It so happened that the well was almost dry, and now she was lying at the bottom with a broken leg.

Cho quickly called for help and in a short time the girl was brought out and given medical care. When the girl

Captain Kazuko, daughter of Commissioner Hasegawa, greets General Erik Wickberg in Norway

After the Commissioner's promotion to Glory, Mrs. Hasegawa, daughter and grand-daughter keep the flag flying

returned from hospital, Cho asked if she could be brought to her room so that she might care for her until she was fully recovered and could walk again. Cho felt special responsibility for her. God had used her to save this young girl from physical death, perhaps He would use her to save her from spiritual death as well. For weeks Cho spent all her spare time with this young, distressed girl. Together they talked through the evening hours. The girl opened her heart to Cho and told her of the sordid life she had been forced to live because of poverty and want, of the debasement and despair of body and soul that had driven her to try to end her life. She saw no purpose in living. Her wound of degradation was too deep. She would never again feel able to live a respectable life or regain her self-respect.

Cho told her of Jesus and of His compassion for the woman who had committed adultery. He had saved her from the hand of her accusers and given her new hope and confidence, as He had said: ' Neither do I condemn thee: go, and sin no more.'

As the young girl listened to Cho's words, she found hope for a new life, a life cleansed by the forgiveness of Jesus. She accepted Him as her Saviour, and strength came to her to live life anew by the help of the Holy Spirit.

A new understanding came to Cho during these evening talks. Having lived a sheltered life in a middle-class, respectable family, she had not imagined such degradation possible, such heartache, such dark despair. She realized how narrow her own thinking had been, how shallow her love for other people, simply because she had not understood them and their circumstances.

After this experience Cho's whole attitude to her work among the women in the home changed, and when, after two years, she received Farewell Orders from Headquarters in Tokyo, she was sorry to say goodbye.

Chapter
Six

HASEGAWA CATCHES THE BUTTERFLY

KOSHI HASEGAWA left his teaching post at the nautical school on Okinajima island in August 1929 for the Salvation Army Training College, in Tokyo. Before leaving he called the twelve-year-old son of the family where he had been boarding, and made a drawing of his foot, promising the lad he would buy him a pair of city shoes when he got to Tokyo, and would post them to him. The country people at that time wore only the high-stepped wooden *getas*, a Japanese version of clogs.

This action was typical of Hasegawa, thoughtful for others and trying to bring happiness where he could into other people's lives. The boy would proudly wear his shiny black shoes and think of the teacher who had remembered him so kindly, the Christian teacher who always spoke about a loving God.

Captain Tamiko Yamamuro, daughter of Commissioner Yamamuro, was on the college staff when Hasegawa entered training and, although there were seventy cadets that year, she remembers Hasegawa well, a tall, handsome man, sitting usually on the back row, looking more like an officer than a cadet. He was studious and alert, always ready to help younger cadets with any problem, whether academic or spiritual. He entered wholeheartedly into the various activities, sold *The War Cry*, visited the people in their homes, preached the gospel with fervour whether on the streets or in Army halls.

The following year he was appointed Cadet-Sergeant,

which meant he remained at the college for a further year with special duties. In his quiet unobtrusive way he helped the newcomers to settle in to the new life; he encouraged the shy and awkward, using discipline fairly, when that was necessary. He quickly won their respect and affection because he was always ready to listen. They found it easy to confide in him, whether it was their personal problems or uncertainty concerning doctrine.

One afternoon Tamiko Yamamuro saw him go down a manhole at the back of the college. It had been blocked up and he was draining it. It was unpleasant work and hard labour too; but rather than ask someone else, Hasegawa chose to do it himself. She realized the extent of his humility of spirit.

After a year as Cadet-Sergeant, Hasegawa became a Captain and was appointed to the college staff. His experience as teacher made him invaluable to the training college. Candidates were drawn from all walks of life, the son of a Greek Orthodox priest, a daughter of a Buddhist priest, college graduates, farmers and artisans; all came with the one purpose of being trained in Salvation Army ' warfare '. The majority of them were brought up in Buddhist and Shinto homes, converted to Christianity in their early youth, and were now eager to spread the gospel of Christ.

The same year as Captain Hasegawa was appointed to the staff of the college, Captain Yamamuro received farewell orders, and in her place came Captain Saito Cho from Osaka Women's Home.

Cho San had, by this time, learnt to love her work among the unfortunate girls and women at the home and in a way was sorry to leave. On the other hand she was naturally excited at the thought of being one of the staff on the training college. It was an appointment after her own heart, for she loved teaching. She also liked being at the centre of things, and above all she revelled in being out among people telling the Good News.

Captain Hasegawa and Captain Saito Cho had worked together at the college for nearly three years, when one day he asked for an interview with the Training Principal. He had a special request. Would the Principal ask Captain Saito Cho if she would marry Captain Hasegawa? Hasegawa was then thirty-three years of age, and Cho thirty-two. Hasegawa was but following the right procedure for proposing to a woman of that day and generation in Japan. There had to be *nakodo*, a go-between. At least this method has the advantage of 'saving face' if the proposal is refused! It is reckoned that today at least 20 per cent of all marriages in the country are thus arranged. Even in 'love marriages' a 'go between' is selected to help with all arrangements. When Salvation Army officers marry, the *nakodo* is usually the Training College Principal, the Divisional Commander or other senior officer.

Marriage in the East is based on suitability more than romance. There is an old saying: 'In the West the man marries the woman he loves; in the East the man loves the woman he marries.'

In The Salvation Army the world over, an officer cannot marry anyone other than an officer, if he or she wishes to remain in the Army as an officer. It happens, of course, that a young officer falls in love with someone outside the ranks but, in order to marry, that person will have to fulfil certain conditions and go through a two years' training course—in fact, become an officer. Theirs is a calling demanding complete dedication and only when husband and wife share the same convictions can they make an equal team.

Captain Hasegawa, having watched Cho San for three years, was sure she had all the virtues for a good marriage. Her temperament and character would complement his own. Where he was quiet and of an introspective nature, she was lively and outgoing; he was patient, she was impetuous; he was studious, she was practical. The two contrasts would complement each other and become a strength to them in their union.

Cho received the proposal of marriage, through the Training College Principal, without much heart flutter. None the less, with womanly instinct, she regarded having a husband and children as the ideal state in life; although, if she could serve her Lord better by remaining single, she would gladly have done so. She prayed about the proposal and accepted, as God's will, that she marry Captain Hasegawa. Of her ability to become a good wife she was not at all sure, but vowed to herself: 'Even if I can't be much help to my husband, I will, at least, never be a hindrance.' As it happened she became a constant strength, always at his side, seeing to his physical needs, tending him in sickness, giving him assurance and confidence.

But marriage could not be for them as yet. Hasegawa's old enemy, ill-health, was getting the better of him. For him to keep fit was a constant battle; but right through life he never allowed any indisposition to hinder his work, never made any allowance for himself, and worked harder than most. With the rigours of campaigning and the heavy schedule of college life, his old chest trouble recurred. Forced to take sick leave, he returned to his brother's home in Kobe to recuperate. He was there from March until November 1934, after which he resumed his duties at the training college.

Meanwhile, Cho, although of a strong constitution, also suffered a physical breakdown. Her intense nature forced her to be always on the go, and being headstrong she would heed no warning. Eventually, much to her displeasure, she had to obey doctor's orders and take complete rest.

Her buoyant spirit soon returned however, and when declared fit for work, she was appointed to take charge of Kumamoto Corps, in the southern island of Kyushu, the place from which her family had emigrated when she was nine years of age.

Captain Saito Cho did splendid work there and is remembered with affection by people whom she led to Christ, and who are still faithful soldiers of the Cross these many years after.

Captain Hasegawa's engagement to Cho was put off because of sickness, but she cherished her promise to marry him. Yet, three years went by without their seeing each other, and they were not youngsters!

When Mrs. Hasegawa sat in my home in Tokyo telling me of her life, I asked about those three years of waiting, a time which to us romantics would have seemed an eternity of agony separated from the loved one.

' Did you still want to marry Captain Hasegawa? '

' Oh yes ', she replied in her brisk, matter-of-fact way, ' but I had to wait.'

' Surely you wrote to each other, even though you couldn't meet during those years? '

' Oh, no, we wouldn't do that. You see, we weren't officially engaged because of sickness, so we couldn't write. That would have been against the rule.'

Her officer-daughter, Mrs. Captain Harita Kazuko, acting as translator between Mrs. Hasegawa and me, saw incredulity written on my face at her mother's statement, so smilingly she said:

' My husband and I also kept the rule. We didn't write to each other while he was in the training college in Australia and I in the training college in England, until our engagement became official.'

Yet, theirs was a love match, self-chosen partners, and still they were prepared to keep the rules and to wait. These dear law-abiding people, are prepared to fit in to a pattern, instead of exerting their own will, happy to keep the rules of the game, willing to sink their own feelings for the greater good, if thereby harmony be produced as a whole. Is this one of the reasons for Japan's greatness?

When both Hasegawa and Cho were back in their respective appointments, the one in Tokyo, the other in Kyushu, the Field Secretary, who is responsible for all corps officers, ascertained that Cho was still willing to marry Captain Hasegawa. The engagement was made official. They started corresponding and six months later, on February 3, 1936, Captain Koshi Hasegawa and Captain Cho Saito were united in marriage under the Army flag. The ceremony was conducted by Lieut.-Colonel Victor Rolfe, at that time joint-Territorial Commander with Lieut.-Colonel Yasowo Segawa. The setting was the corps hall at Kanda, where Hasegawa, as a young student, had knelt and decided to follow Christ.

So on their wedding day, Koshi and Cho took their place on the platform facing the congregation. This in itself was symbolic. They faced the world, so to speak; their union was not sought for the sake of their own happiness and interest only, but the better to serve God, and more earnestly to seek to spread the gospel. Part of their solemn declaration was: 'We promise that we will use all our influence with each other to promote our constant and entire self-sacrifice in fighting in the ranks of the Army for the salvation of the world.' Solemn words indeed!

Right through life, the Hasegawas kept their marriage vows, not only to each other, but to the world. Many have been blessed through their united endeavours.

There was no wedding ring—they were too poor for that, although they observed Japanese tradition in giving to each of the wedding guests a gift. There was no honeymoon—life was too earnest!

It may not have been a 'love match' at that time, but

both brought to their marriage loyalty and respect. These qualities are strong, stronger even than 'falling in love', yet not as strong as love, for love is above all else.

Fond of flowers, of green fields and shaded woods, all Hasegawa's years as a Salvation Army officer were spent in the great city of Tokyo, surrounded by steel and concrete. To make up for lack of natural beauty he kept, both in his home and office, pot plants which he tended with utmost care.

After his death these became Mrs. Hasegawa's greatest treasures. One day, two-and-a-half years after he had died she told me that the cyclamen was in full bloom and had forty-eight flowers. She had counted each one!

So in like manner, as Hasegawa and his wife shared life together, respect and loyalty blossomed into love which endured to the very end.

*Chapter
Seven*

HASEGAWA AS HUSBAND AND FATHER

MAN has an exalted position in Japan. Even in this age when Japan has opened wide her doors to other influences through inter-travel, cinema and television, little has changed in the man-woman relationship, although there are doubtless more ' love marriages '. By and large, man's position as lord and master is still indisputable, yet, strange as it may seem—the wife keeps the purse!

Fortunate is the Japanese woman whose husband expresses tender affection by passing things to her at the table before helping himself, or who knows the pleasant feeling of importance when sweeping first through a door kept open by a courteous male companion. Somehow, the Japanese woman seems to find compensation by letting her male companion take the seat in a crowded train or bus, while she stands happily fanning his heated brow.

While in the eyes of a woman from the West her Japanese sister's position would seem unenviable, the Japanese woman is by no means unhappy. She accepts the situation which, to a certain degree, is of her own making, in the way she has brought up her sons to expect to be served, using womanly guile to win her own point if and when she deems it necessary!

A Japanese wife finds pleasure in looking after her husband and takes great pride in his appearance. It is doubtful whether in any other country in the world one finds such immaculately dressed men as in Japan.

Has the Japanese woman a greater capacity for self-forgetfulness than her Western counterpart? It is difficult to say, but she most certainly finds it easier to accept life than do many women in the Occident who seem to think it owes them happiness.

The newly-married Mrs. Hasegawa was quite prepared to serve her husband in the tradition of the country, though it can hardly be said by natural inclination. But she was in for a few surprises. Her husband did not want to be served! As a sailor he had learnt self-reliance; he could cook, clean and darn his socks as well as any woman. His training had served him well in a long bachelor existence teaching in the nautical school and later at the Salvation Army Training College. Personally he could not see why a wife should do all the menial tasks and wait on her husband. To him marriage was partnership; and especially in The Salvation Army where both husband and wife had been commissioned as Salvation Army officers.

So Captain Hasegawa happily took part in house cleaning, lifting the heavy *futons* (bedding) from the *tatami* floors each morning, placing them in the wall cupboard, and again spreading them out on the floor at night. He even 'did' the dishes, washed his own socks and underwear, a most un-Japanese thing for a man to do, and most amazing of all—he even cleaned his wife's shoes!

It was amusing to see the reaction to Hasegawa's domestic prowess among other Japanese. That others thought it queer never embarrassed him. He was never in a hurry to discard his apron for any caller, even if they might consider he was lowering himself.

Major Tateishi, an officer working at Territorial Headquarters in Tokyo, gives her early observations:

'When I began to work at the Salvation Army clinic in Kanda I did not know anything about The Salvation Army, nor about Christianity. Everything was new and strange. Captain Hasegawa and his family lived in one part of the training college building in Harajuku. Another part was used as a women students' hostel. Four of us, working in the clinic at Kanda, lived at the hostel. We all used the same kitchen, officers and students alike.

'One night I was eating my supper in the dining hall, and along came Captain Hasegawa, with a saucepan, and his three children, each carrying plates and cups and a kettle. When we saw them there the first time we were all very surprised because we were not used to seeing the man, the head of the house, helping to wash the dishes after dinner. The students, who came from the country and had known only feudalistic society, were particularly surprised to see the Captain. Gradually, we all got used to it, it taught us practical democracy. Later on I was converted to Christianity and became a Salvationist.'

Like his Master, Hasegawa had come to serve, not to be served, and for him no task was too humble. He kept this spirit of humility right through life, no elevation in rank or position made any difference to him. He was always a humble servant of Christ. To him humility and sincerity were of equal importance, and he practised both.

The old saying, previously quoted, 'Earthquake, lightning, fire and fathers are to be feared', does not really apply any longer. When travelling about in Japan these days one often sees a young father carrying the baby, or humouring a little toddler in patience and love. But, in the early days of Hasegawa's married life, he was probably a trend-setter of a new pattern of fatherhood.

When Hasegawa and Cho married he was thirty-six and she a year younger, so there was not much time to spare for starting a family. Within the next four years, Mrs. Hasegawa presented her husband with three lovely, healthy children: Hiroshi, a son, and two daughters, Kazuko and Kiyoko.

As they grew up, the bond of affection between parents

and children increased with the years. Hasegawa seldom scolded his family. He regarded them as rational beings, even when they were quite young, and always appealed to their common sense.

Kazuko, the elder of the two girls, remembers one hot summer's day when she was very young. Because of the heat she felt terribly thirsty and, forgetting all the good manners her mother had taught her, she grabbed a teapot standing on a low table and started drinking out of the spout. Father, sitting writing in a corner of the room, noticed what was going on. Instead of shouting at her, he rose quietly, took the teapot from her and said: ' If that tea had been hot you would have scalded yourself.'

The little girl avoided looking up at her father; she did not want to see his displeasure.

Another time Hiroshi, the brother, and the two girls were playing together in the small living room. A Japanese room with low ceiling, rice-paper doors and low hanging lamp is hardly at any time a suitable playground for children. The three of them had picked up brooms and were marching up and down, making a terrific din. The inevitable happened. A broom landed in the lamp which splintered into many pieces. Just then father arrived on the scene. There was silence. The children wondered what to expect—a feeling of guilt written on their young faces. All they received was a gentle admonishment, telling them that if any glass splinters had gone into their eyes they would have become blind. A fearsome thought, far more dreadful than any scolding or threat of punishment! His method was effective; he expected them to use their powers of reasoning and, young as they were, they responded to it.

While the children were small and Captain Hasegawa was working at Headquarters, Mrs. Hasegawa would take the children every morning and walk to the station, pushing the pram, to see father off. These walks with father the children used to prize, for more often than not they would be asleep by the time he returned home in the evening. He was in the habit of working late.

When they were a little older he delegated more time to the children's education. He taught them to play the piano, until their piano was destroyed by a bomb during the war. On special occasions he took them to concerts to develop in them the same love of music which meant so much to him. During the Christmas season they were taken to hear Handel's *Messiah*, always performed in Tokyo and other big cities in Japan during the month of December. With an audience of a thousand or more, mostly non-Christian, they listened spellbound to the singing. Just before the choir started the ' Hallelujah Chorus ', father would tell them to stand up straight, and there they stood in awesome reverence with everyone —Christian and non-Christian alike—while the tremendous words filled the concert hall: 'And He shall reign for ever and ever, King of kings and Lord of lords! Hallelujah!'

Hasegawa lived a life of discipline and simplicity. Rising early every morning, in the hot summer months as well as in the winter when the temperature was at freezing point, he would rub down his body with cold water. After a time spent in Bible-reading and meditation, he would give his wife a hand with domestic chores and, after breakfast, leave for the office. Returning home at night he would put away his Army uniform and don the traditional Japanese kimono and sit cross-legged on the *tatami* floor. In the office he would be no different from any other Salvation Army officer working at International Headquarters in London or any other Headquarters round the world; at home he would be Japanese to the core.

The kimono and the uniform, as wearing apparel, may represent East and West, but it was no split-level existence for Hasegawa, who felt as much at home in his uniform as in his kimono. For him there was no East or West, for he belonged, with all his heart, to the world-wide Salvation Army.

In his short hours of leisure he would take to brush writing. The *kakemono*, or hanging scroll, takes the place of framed pictures. Often it contains some valued calligraphy, for in Japan calligraphic skill is no less esteemed than skill in painting. With a sure, artistic sense he wielded the brush and produced letters of distinction. On scrolls he wrote that which to him was of pre-eminent importance in life, the very essence of the law of life in Christ: ' Love one another ', ' Continue in My love ', ' Faith, hope and love '. In this way Hasegawa spread the message of love far and wide. Not only in many homes in Japan are his brush writings on the walls, but in homes across the seas. To newly-married officers he would write the words: ' Christ is the Head of this home.'

When a woman with knowledge of the art of brush writing saw one of his scrolls she said: ' This is not done by a professional brush-writer, but by someone with a deep feeling for the words, for the letters are alive.' To many recipients of Hasegawa's brush writing, the message of God's love became alive.

As the children grew up they had in their father a wonderful example of Christian living, someone to whom they could go with their problems.

Kazuko was worried because, although she loved God and considered herself a Christian, she could not date a specific time in her life when she had decided to follow Christ and accept His forgiveness of sins. She spoke to her father about it. He opened his Bible and pointed to Paul's letter to the Romans, chapter eight, verse sixteen: ' The Spirit itself beareth witness with our spirit, that we are the children of God.' He then explained to his young daughter: ' If you have asked Jesus to forgive you your sins and you know within your own heart that you love

HASEGAWA AS HUSBAND AND FATHER

Him and want to do His will—then you know that you are saved.'

Later, when Kazuko was in training for officership at the International Training College in London, she wrote to her father and confessed that her ideas of holiness did not seem to tally with some of the teaching she received. To her it seemed that holiness could be attained only through constant growth.

He wrote back to his daughter carefully explaining the eternal truths from his own experience in Christian living: ' Holiness is indeed growth in Christlikeness and takes a lifetime, but first there must be a complete surrender of self. When we come to God for pardon we may not then realize the need for full commitment. Only when our will is made one with His will can we know the fullness of His blessings. Sanctification is God's seal upon our lives by His Holy Spirit.'

He finished his letter by referring to Paul's letter to the Ephesians, chapter one, verses thirteen and fourteen: ' In Him you also, who have heard the word of truth, the gospel of your salvation, and have believed in Him, were sealed with the promised Holy Spirit, which is the guarantee of our inheritance until we acquire possession of it, to the praise of His glory.'

Hiroshi and Kiyoko, the son and younger daughter, have written about their father in retrospect. Hiroshi, secretary to a Member of Parliament, speaks discerningly, as a man weighing up another man, but the fact that the man was his father shines through in his love for him:

' My father was a genuine Christian, who saw everything through the light of God. He was loyal to God, thrilled at others experiencing a sense of guilt, and gave himself to the task of salvation. He was most happy when he could feel an indirect heavenly joy; but he looked remorseful and rather disdainful when having to work out human problems. Whenever he was forced to succeed in anything mundane he became perplexed; partly because he was not sure at the outset whether or not the human goal was in line with Providence, and partly because success or failure was in God's hands eventually.

' My father was a noble spirit. But he was a man who had to live with despair. He once told me that he had forsaken the world when he watched on the spot the death of his best friend, who fell from the top of the main mast on board ship. He graduated from the college with honours, but he was constrained to accept a comparatively easy teaching post in order to cure tuberculosis. Under the guidance of his elder sister he became a Christian. And when he was twenty-eight, on New Year's eve, he saw Jesus at the height of an earnest prayer.

' My father once told me that the person he loved best was his deceased mother. (She died when he was forty-five years old.) He was handsome and women were kind to him. He was proud of his daughters and the greatest satisfaction he ever had was that his daughter, Kazuko, devoted herself to the work of God.

' I loved my father when he was alive, but it was only when I lost him that I realized he had loved me. Yes, he loved me and he loves me.

' They might call me an agnostic; but I don't mind that. Since I have a conviction to the effect that I can and must meet my father, Hasegawa Koshi, some day together with my wife and daughter, I am already beyond and above this world.'

Kiyoko was fortunate to share with her father a love of nature, which she describes:

' I loved to listen to my father speaking of the days when he was on the training ship as a student. It was thrilling to imagine what kind of countries were over the ocean, and how that little ship could plough through the rough waves in stormy weather. When father spoke about the sea and the ship, he looked so happy. He told me that they made astronomical observations in order to know the location of ships. He had a machine for that purpose at home. He used to say that he would like to observe the stars when he retired from active service in The Salvation Army, and really he was looking forward to it. Often we went out into the garden on summer nights and father taught us the constellations. Sometimes we would go up to the roof of the training college at Harakuku and we would observe the moon through his telescope.

'Later on, when I began doing skin-diving, I became much more interested in the state of the sky. The sea is not always calm and nice for us to enjoy, so it is necessary to forecast the weather beforehand. When I was out in the garden to check the movement of the clouds and the direction of the wind, and at the same time to enjoy the marvellous cloud effect in the autumnal sky, or the sunset colours, father, too, would come out into the garden after the day's work and teach me about the weather.

'We realize some of the splendour of nature when we look up at the sky, but more so if we go into the sea. The calm sea is wonderful. How can those small fish live in dark and deep waters, and why do they wear such various kinds of clothes, even though no one is looking at them? When I watched them in the quiet and noiseless world, I found peace of heart. But when it was stormy the sea resisted everybody, everything. However much we fought, the sea could squeeze us easily. I experienced the great power of nature.

'I remember once father looking up at the sky, but I think he was looking further than the sky. I think he was trying to tell me that a man is only a little helpless being in this great universe. Several days after my father died I saw a great rainbow. It was the most perfect rainbow I have ever seen. It reminded me of my father.'

Chapter
Eight

WAR CLOUDS GATHER

HASEGAWA was proud of the Army to which he belonged—
' Save-the-World Army '. Prior to his marriage he had been appointed to Territorial Headquarters as secretary to the Territorial Commander and Chief Secretary. To work closely with Commissioner Yamamuro was a great joy. He was the man whose words had compelled him to become a Christian and who later had encouraged him in his decision to become a Salvation Army officer; a man whose Christianity was vital and fearless, and whose enthusiasm for the Kingdom he, Hasegawa, wanted to emulate.

From the reports that came to Headquarters from the many centres of Army activity throughout Japan he learned of the tremendous progress that had been made in the forty years the Army had been in operation in his country. There was now a staff of 512 active and retired officers, with 147 corps, 160 outposts and 25 institutions.

The 1936 *Salvation Army Year Book* gives a graphic picture of those days:

' Sixty-eight cadets completed their training and were commissioned as officers. Some were retained for further training in accordance with the recently inaugurated two-year training system. Many parents oppose their children entering training for Salvation Army officership. Some disinherit them; others follow them to the garrison determined to carry them off for a final family council, but in many cases, before the ' family council ' stage is reached, the parents or relatives find themselves in the Training Principal's office, weeping over and confessing their sins.

When this happens the parents gladly offer their children for officership.

' Thousands of seekers were registered during the year, representing many more thousands who were brought into contact with the gospel message through the Army's evangelistic meetings, open-airs, publications, home league and young people's and other organized activities. One month was specially devoted to open-air campaigning, and corps officers report many instances of drumhead conversions.

' Social institutions include a tuberculosis sanatorium, a general hospital and three medical dispensaries, two rescue homes for women, one home for children of lepers; a slum settlement and a day nursery; one home for adolescent girls; two homes for juvenile offenders; two children's homes; one ex-prisoners' home, three working men's homes, two free shelters for men; one farm, one students' hostel.

' The Sunamachi free shelter for men opened an industrial wing where paper-sorting, glove-making, and other such work is undertaken. The Tamagawa farm sent a group of men (mostly Salvationists) to Manchukuo, where they settled under a Government scheme. A home for girls and a new rescue home for women were other acquisitions during 1935. Most of the latter was donated by Mr. Kenzo Sato, brother of the late Mrs. Commissioner Yamamuro, in compliance with a youthful promise to his sister, that when he became a successful business man he would donate Yen 100.00. The promise has now been fulfilled one hundredfold.'

And in 1938: ' Several hundred children from Tokyo's canal barges were the recipients of gifts at Christmas-time. As every year, a free winter shelter was opened in Tokyo, accommodating over 100 of the most destitute men. These include illiterates and men of education, unemployed, dustbin-scavengers, drink addicts and gamblers and others.

'A gift from Her Majesty the Empress provided these men with a special meal. Her Imperial Majesty also sent a donation for our free dispensary work in Tokyo, while H.I.H. Prince Chichibu manifested his interest in our activities by personally inspecting our Tamagawa farm, where he was received by Commissioner Yamamuro.'

The future looked bright for the Christian cause in Japan; but on the horizon clouds of opposition were gathering. The country had risen from an isolated, obscure state to a world power in a short time. Japan had become a highly technical and advanced nation; but, with industrial progress, came also political unrest.

The idea of the Emperor of Japan being regarded as a god is generally known. What is not generally known is that he had risen to such eminence only within the last century and through political manoeuvre. Although his ' divinity ' goes back to the dawn of Japan's history, which hails the first ruler of the country as the son of the sun goddess, and only a descendant of this ' divine ' line could govern the people as Emperor, for centuries Japan had been ruled by feudal lords, with the Emperor merely a ' shadowy figurehead '.

According to Ruth Benedict's book, *The Chrysanthemum and the Sword*, the Emperor was without actual power and his financial resources were smaller than those of even lesser *daimyos* (feudal lords); even the royal ceremonies were strictly circumscribed by Shogunate regulations (*The Generalissimo*). When Commodore Perry arrived in Japan, he did not even suspect the existence of an Emperor, and the first American envoy, Townsend Harris, who negotiated the first commercial treaty with Japan in 1858, had to discover for himself that there was an Emperor.

How then did it come to pass that the people grew to regard the Emperor as ' divine ' and swore to him their allegiance, even to sacrificing their lives?

WAR CLOUDS GATHER

We have already seen that in 1868 the Emperor became active ruler of the country and, bringing about the ' Meiji Restoration ', transformed Japan into a strong military and industrial power. Edwin O. Reischauer, eminent historian and at one time U.S. Ambassador to Japan, explains the phenomenon in *Japan Past and Present*: ' The Meiji leaders, who had come to power by championing the right of the Emperor to rule, had created and fostered this tradition—the mystic position of the Emperor as a demi-god whose personal will, in theory, took precedence over all law. This gave them, as the men who surrounded the throne and spoke for the Emperor, far greater authority over the people than they could have achieved otherwise.'

In fact, the military was in control, both over the civil government, as well as over Japan's foreign policies. Military leaders wanted to expand Japan's territory and make room for their increasing population; capitalists wanted raw material for the country's flourishing factories.

The Japanese people have a strong sense of obligation and loyalty; to do one's duty is of utmost importance to them. Of this characteristic of their people military leaders took full advantage and indoctrinated them, through the mass media, to swear allegiance to the country and Emperor. ' In fulfilling these obligations ', the nation was told, ' all other obligations were fulfilled ', and so the people were trained in obedience to the Emperor and to the army, as the visible symbol of imperial might and authority.

Although aggression can never be condoned, or called anything but evil, if our condemnation weigh stronger against one nation than another, we do well to remember that Japan does not stand alone as aggressor. Many an empire has been built up through aggression.

In October 1941 General Tojo, head of the army,

became also Prime Minister. A period of indoctrination swept the country in schools and colleges and through the mass media. Textbooks were constantly revised to bring them in line with the spirit of the time. Great devotion was expressed to the 'imperial will' and slogans such as 'East Asia for the East Asiatics', 'The East Asiatic Co-Prosperity Sphere', and 'the Japanese spirit' were heard everywhere. Anything 'un-Japanese' was frowned upon. Westerners were observed with suspicion and as possible spies. Japan sent its armies into China, Korea and Manchuria.

An incident comes to mind illustrating the inconstancy of worldly power. It happened in 1972 in the northern island of Hokkaido in a town called Otaru. A meeting had been arranged for Salvation Army officers of the island, in a Government tourist centre, a beautiful, old building in traditional Japanese style, situated on a hill jutting into Otaru Bay, part of the Japan Sea.

The small group of officers had come from isolated places, where they preached with great zeal the gospel of Christ to non-Christians, and cared for their little flock of Salvationists. We sat on cushions by a low table with lacquer top; through the half-open sliding doors of delicately patterned rice-paper we could see the blue sea flecked with white, as sailing boats glided to and fro in the breeze.

On one of the walls hung an ornate plaque which drew our attention. When the meeting was over my husband asked a young officer what was written on this interesting-looking plaque covered with elaborate, flourished letters. For some time he studied it with knitted brow, then turning to us with an apologetic smile said: ' I'm sorry, I can't read it; the letters are so old-fashioned and not in use today.'

Behind him stood an old, retired woman officer. In soft-spoken words, hardly audible she started to recite. Then

WAR CLOUDS GATHER

she said: 'When I was a child we started every day at school by reciting this. By so doing we swore allegiance to the Emperor.'

Times have changed. Not only are the words forgotten by younger generations; they cannot even read the text, for Japan's written language has changed. From impressions one gets of the Emperor, he in no way misses the former adulation given him. A quiet, reserved man he is more interested, it would seem, in his studies of marine biology than in being a demi-god.

At a time when nationalism was exalted, it was to be expected that an international organization such as The Salvation Army would meet difficulties. Certain officers within Salvation Army ranks were influenced by the prevailing spirit and wanted to break away from International Headquarters in London and establish an independent Japanese Salvation Army. National feelings ran high, creating friction within the Movement; but by far the majority of officers and soldiers remained loyal and stood their ground, although they felt, at times, that the pressure within was harder to bear than the pressure from without. Their loyalty was above all earthly loyalty because their allegiance was to God.

Through all the tragic years that followed they remained true to God, true to The Salvation Army which had been the instrument in leading them to God, and true to the General, as international leader of the Army; for they believed that The Salvation Army stood for universal brotherhood, one God, Father of all, and all mankind His children, of whatever race or country.

In 1938 Hasegawa was saddened when Commissioner Yamamuro, for a second time, had to relinquish his position as Territorial Commander. The passing of his beloved wife and the constant pressure of present circumstances caused a further breakdown in health. The reins of responsibility were passed to Colonel Masuzo Uyemura, with Lieutenant-Colonel Yasowo Segawa as Chief Secretary, both outstanding Japanese officers, while Commissioner Yamamuro, in capacity as Territorial Counsellor, gave support and advice. Captain Hasegawa remained in the appointment of secretary to the Territorial Commander, and at the same time continued as Yamamuro's trusted English correspondent.

Lieut.-Colonel Tamiko Yamamuro gives a glimpse of references to Hasegawa in her father's diary which, during his illness was entered by someone else:

> July 30th, 1938. We had a cable from London. It looks like a very serious matter. Commissioner let Captain Hasegawa write a letter and send it by express delivery.

World events at that time gave cause for great anxiety. War clouds were gathering. The difficulty of keeping communications open between International Headquarters in London and Japan was considerable if war should flare up.

> April 19th, 1939. The General wrote about the High Council. Captain Hasegawa was told to write that the Commissioner was not able to attend the Council.

Again Hasegawa was saddened at the increased frailty of his beloved leader.

At the High Council, the Territorial Commander, Lieut.-Commissioner Uyemura, represented Japan. Meeting international leaders from all parts of the world at this crucial time in history was a source of constant strength to Japan's leader in the agonizing years that were to follow. The bond of internationalism was strengthened and friendships then formed held, when hatred and violence chained other men in their grip. General George Carpenter remembered with sympathy and affection his Japanese comrade-officer when by force of circumstance he had to sever links with London.

On March 13, 1940 Commissioner Yamamuro was promoted to Glory, his passing mourned by high and low.

WAR CLOUDS GATHER

He was a remarkably gifted man, who had given all his talents to God to be used for the good of the people. His *Common People's Gospel* lives on long after his voice has ceased to speak. In spite of growing opposition and adverse feelings against The Salvation Army as an international body, Yamamuro's name was honoured by the Imperial Household: the Emperor, Empress and the Dowager Empress presented a consolation gift for the funeral, sealed with the royal seal. This was of great encouragement to all Salvationists who felt the strain of antagonism.

However, suspicion against The Salvation Army, as a ' foreign ' organization grew among Government officials and only a few days after Yamamuro's passing *The Common People's Gospel* was banned. A copy of the book, coming into the hands of an unsympathetic Diet member, was banned by Government as subversive literature. Headquarters was commanded to send letters to all officers throughout Japan who had copies for sale in their corps. Every copy was to be destroyed, not one must remain. Instead, many put their supply in boxes and buried them in the ground, thereby exposing themselves to severe punishment if discovered. But thousands and thousands of copies of this book, with its plain gospel teaching had already been sold, and its eternal truth lived on in many hearts during those dark days.

The following is interesting to note: ' In 1962 the French government asked Japanese authorities to recommend four leading social workers from the last 150 years. In consultation with the Ministry of Health and Welfare, the Japanese Ministry of Foreign Affairs submitted resource material on four men. Commissioner Yamamuro was one of those four.'

Today Yamamuro's books are found in public libraries in Japan and children in school learn about his life and literature.

As the day of Japanese involvement in the Second World War grew nearer, greater pressure was put on Salvationists. Officers were under suspicion of acting as spies and their homes were searched. Lieut.-Commissioner Uyemura and Colonel Segawa were arrested and taken to the military prison for interrogation, but released, after ten days, when nothing could be found against them. Headquarters files and books were taken for inspection by the military. Adverse criticism of The Salvation Army was printed in newspapers. People started to eye Salvationists with suspicion and contempt wherever they went. Often when travelling by train, or other public transport, officers endured the humiliation of being searched and having their diaries and papers scrutinized by military police, who hoped to find some word which would reveal them as disloyal citizens. They were confronted with the question: 'Who is the greater—our Emperor or your foreign God?'

Inevitably, overseas officers had to leave the country at that time. Major Victor Rich, the Financial Secretary, and his wife, the only remaining overseas officers, were ordered to report daily to military authorities and eventually expelled from the country. Wearing private clothes, Tamiko, the daughter of Commissioner Yamamuro, and Colonel Segawa accompanied them to the docks in Yokohama, and with their departure the last physical link with the outside Salvationist world was broken.

Finally the authorities forced Lieut.-Commissioner Uyemura and Colonel Segawa to send a cable to International Headquarters severing all connections with London. The words in the cable had, by stress of circumstance, to be short and guarded. There was no way of explaining, no possibility of voicing the distress felt by this inevitable step; no way to pledge the loyalty of thousands of Japanese Salvationists to the common cause, however adverse the circumstances. They would have to hide the Salvation Army flag, their international banner, but they believed the day would dawn when once again they would be able to unfurl it. They would remain true until that day.

A reply telegram from General Carpenter was received with intense relief. He had understood the unspoken words. His Christ-like attitude moved the Salvation Army leaders of Japan deeply. The General expressed gratitude to Japanese Salvationists and urged them to trust in God and keep on praying.

Circumstances changed from day to day; more and more restrictions were enforced. The name ' Salvation Army' proved distasteful to military leaders, only one army would be allowed in Japan and that the military army. So the Movement's name was changed from *Kyu Sei Gun* (Save-the-World Army), to *Kyu Sei Dan* (Save-the-World Group). Other Army vocabulary had to be altered. ' Soldier ' was no longer to be used; ' believer ' was put in its place.

The War Cry had to have another title. For a short time it was published under the name *Nihon Kyu Sei Shinbun*, in English, *Japan Save-the-World Newspaper*. Then that, also, was anathema and amended to *Asa no Hikari* (*Morning Light*). All too soon that had also to be discontinued.

Chapter
Nine

RAVAGES OF WAR AND RESTORATION

On June 27, 1940, Captain Hasegawa was appointed to take charge of Omori Corps and, with his wife and young family, moved their few belongings to the corps quarters in the suburb in the southern part of Tokyo. But this appointment did not last long, for after less than four months came yet another upheaval when the family had to move back to the training college, where Hasegawa again took up a position on the staff. In this critical period, when the future was uncertain, Hasegawa, with his calm disposition, unruffled and composed at all times, yet with a firm will to do the right, was a great strength to Brigadier Rintaro Watanabe, the Training Principal.

That a college where young people were trained to become Salvation Army officers, would be affected by the many military impositions, was to be expected. The name *Kyu Sei Gakuin* (Save-the-World College) became *Toko Gakuin* (East Light College).

There were twenty cadets in the college that year—ten men and ten women, who, after a year's training, were sent to various appointments throughout the country to gain practical experience, either in evangelistic or social work, and later recalled to the college for further theoretical training before being commissioned as officers.

Only two men and one woman returned. War had started, Japan having thrown herself headlong into the conflict of the second world holocaust. On December 7, 1941, the Japanese Navy attacked Pearl Harbour, and the

RAVAGES OF WAR AND RESTORATION

same month The Salvation Army, then called 'Save-the-World Group', ceased to function in its original form as an independent body. Thirty-four Protestant churches were compelled by Government to form one juridical body known as the *Kyodan* or United Church of Christ in Japan. Registered as number eleven, The Salvation Army became part of the *Kyodan*. The sole other body recognized by the Religious Organizations Law was the Roman Catholic Church.

The sorrow felt by Japanese Salvationists when no longer allowed to wear Salvation Army uniform was great. Many hid their uniforms away to be brought out again, when, as they firmly believed, The Salvation Army would be free once more to function in Japan. Among these were the Hasegawas.

The Territorial Headquarters was taken over by the War Department and the training college put to use as a military medical college.

The three cadets who had returned to college for further training were sent to the Japan Christian Theological College. Hiramoto San, Takehana San, and the young woman, Fukutake San (San—title of address for man or woman, married and unmarried alike). After the war Takehana San married Fukutake San, and it is noteworthy that all three are still officers over thirty years later.

The *Kyodan*, being a church body, would not recognize Salvation Army officers as ministers, because they had not received baptism. This created a problem. A large number of officers accepted the church ruling, were baptized and became ordained pastors; some carried on the work in the corps to which they had been appointed before the dissolution of The Salvation Army. Here they held services on Sundays, often while bombs were dropping, and shepherded their little flock of faithful Christians. During the week they had to work for their living or do national service.

Hasegawa, though gentle of appearance, had a firmness of character allowing no deviation from what he thought right. As he once said to another officer: ' It is better if you give way to others when either point will do. But there are occasions when you have to stick to your own conviction and will not be able to concede your point.'

Hasegawa held the opinion that having been converted, of which baptism is an outward sign, and having pledged himself as a soldier of Christ and been commissioned as a Salvation Army officer, he did not need to receive baptism in order to be an ordained minister in the church.

His belief was clearly summed up in Ephesians 4: 5, 6: ' One Lord, one faith, one baptism, One God and Father of all.' ' The one Lord ' the Lord Jesus; the ' one faith ' faith in the Lord Jesus; the ' one baptism ' the baptism which the Lord Jesus gives. John said: ' He sent me to baptize with water. . . . This is He who baptizes with the Holy Spirit.'

Having received the baptism of the Holy Spirit, that to Hasegawa was enough. He informed the church authorities that he considered his dedication and commission as a Salvation Army officer sufficient authority for him to continue to preach the gospel.

During the war years Hasegawa was set to work in a factory making lenses; but his first interest was to maintain Salvation Army work under whatever name it might be called. Our social institutions and hospitals were still operating, though deprived of the name ' Salvation Army '.

In 1943 a Juridical Foundation called *Nippon Kirisutokyo Airinkai* was established (in English, '*Japan Christian Church Love to Neighbours*') of which Major Mitaro Akimoto, a faithful and loyal officer and gifted writer, was made Director, and Hasegawa General Secretary, with Usui San (later Lieut.-Colonel) responsible for the accounts.

RAVAGES OF WAR AND RESTORATION

With the tempo of war steadily increasing, air raids became daily happenings. A bomb fell in the grounds of the Booth Hospital in Suginami, a suburb of Tokyo, but miraculously did not explode and was removed without causing damage. It was not so at Misujimachi, our other Tokyo hospital, 'The Founder's Memorial Hospital', a three-storey building, of fine reputation, with 160 maternity beds, caring for the wounded during the war.

On March 10, 1944, a fearful day, when much of Tokyo was destroyed, bombs fell and a fire started on the top floor of the hospital building. Feverishly the staff worked to move the patients to safety. Eventually all were gathered on the ground floor—there was nowhere else to go. They expected the worst—yet kept on praying that their lives would be saved. The fire raged. The third floor was burned down; then the second floor likewise. There was not much hope; the heat and the smoke had become unbearable. Then, as by a miracle, the flames subsided just when it seemed as if the first floor would also catch fire. With the fire under control, all the patients and staff were saved.

Mrs. Captain Kawai, whose husband had been called up for military service, was the valiant Head Nurse of the hospital. That night, after seeing to the safety and comfort of the patients, she started out for Kuramae Corps close by. Here she held services in between her duties at the hospital. A few of the faithful having gathered in the small Army hall, she commenced the meeting. Before long fighter bombers blackened the sky overhead. She thought it wisest for all present to seek cover in the nearest air-raid shelter. A direct hit blew up that shelter and the sole identity of this devoted, faithful officer was a small remnant of her uniform skirt, which she had worn with a white blouse—a little square of navy blue serge. Her husband's last appointment was as Chief Secretary for Japan, Colonel Mitsuji Kawai.

The Hasegawas by this time had three small children and to bring them out of immediate danger Mrs. Hasegawa left Tokyo. A friend, knowing a farmer a little way from Tokyo, in the Saitama Prefecture, suggested that Mrs. Hasegawa should take the young family there. The four of them were given one room on the second floor, and they were grateful to be away from the danger of air raids. In the country they did not go hungry as they had done in the city, where food was becoming more and more scarce.

Soon after the family left their home in Takinogawa, Tokyo, that too was destroyed in an air raid. It happened while Hasegawa was at work in the factory. When he returned home at night only a fire smouldered where once the house had stood. For several minutes he watched the smoking debris, wondering if there might be anything to salvage—there was nothing. The broken and scattered strings of his beloved piano sent his thoughts to the many people throughout the world with broken heart strings; the pain within him was almost unbearable. Not for himself did he grieve, but for others; not for his own people alone, but for the many who were suffering because of this evil thing, war.

Now homeless, he thanked God for the safety of his wife and children in the country and made his way to them. Here, for a couple of months, he shared their one room. This meant he had to leave at 5 a.m. to reach the factory in time. The precision work he was set to do called for intense concentration. The hours were long, often as many as twelve a day, and he returned home at night, utterly exhausted.

Later it was arranged for him to share a flat with three other Salvation Army officers at Suginami, next to the Army hospital and nearer his place of work.

Two of these companions were called up and sent to the front. While they were away, both lost their wives: Captain Kawai, who has already been mentioned, and

RAVAGES OF WAR AND RESTORATION

Captain Koyano, who on his return after the war was informed that his wife had died in hospital.

While this story was being written Brigadier Koyano, in Command of Tokyo Division, recalled under considerable emotional stress something of what he had felt during those days. As a Christian he knew war was wrong; he could not hate his enemy, for Christ had told him to love them, and right through those gruelling years his one prayer had been that he would not have to kill anybody—that was his greatest fear—and God answered his prayer.

Hasegawa's keenness in maintaining the work of The Salvation Army, though not so called, never slackened throughout the war years. His Christian witness never faltered; in word and in deed he lived the Christian life. He showed concern for his fellow workers in the factory and, whenever an opportunity was given, spoke to them of Christ. He started a choir among the women workers. They did so well that a concert was arranged and was greatly appreciated by everyone. He was kept busy as secretary of *Airinkai*, the social work which continued to serve the people. He held Bible classes regularly in Kyobashi, a corps situated in the centre of Tokyo, near the famous Ginza. Notwithstanding its strategic position, it was the only Army hall in Tokyo not destroyed during the war, apart from the military-occupied Kanda Central Hall.

Captain Shinichi Yoshida, later Commissioner and Territorial Commander of Japan, was appointed to this corps before the war, and kept up his pastoral work there from the time the Army had to change its name to *Kyu Sei Dan* (Save-the-World Group), remaining after the Army became part of the Japan United Church, till the time when once again the Army flag was unfurled.

During the week Yoshida San worked as a clerk in a Government office; on Sundays he preached the gospel to the people of Kyobashi, and Hasegawa stood by him taking his share in the services. Often military police entered the hall and sat on the back bench, listening to what was being said, making notes, waiting for an opportunity to issue a warrant to the speaker for disloyalty to country and Emperor.

Yoshida's name had been registered for military service; he had no reason to be exempt. Time went on and he received no word from military headquarters, so he continued his work in the office, conducting religious services in Kyobashi, visiting the people, and trying to bring comfort to those mourning the loss of loved ones.

Then one day a letter, bearing the Government seal, was delivered at his house. It was addressed to Mrs. Yoshida. Trembling she opened it and read: ' We regret to inform you of the death of your husband, Yoshida Shinichi, who died in battle.' Enclosed was a cheque, a widow's pension! However, the husband returned home from the office that evening to a confused wife. Even though she knew a mistake had been made somewhere, it had unnerved her to see his name as a war casualty.

The cheque was returned to Military Headquarters and the mistake cleared up. Another Yoshida Shinichi had been killed in battle, and notice had been sent to the wrong wife! It was now clear to Yoshida why he had not been called up; another, by the same name, had done service for him. It was a sobering thought that his life might have ended on a battlefield. Accepting the renewed gift of life from God, he reconsecrated himself to His service.

Soon after this, peace was declared. On August 6 and 9, 1945, atom bombs had fallen on Hiroshima and Nagasaki, wiping out nearly 200,000 lives. The Emperor's voice was heard over the radio telling his people throughout the land that Japan had surrendered. The war was over.

Restoration of Japan was a colossal task. Not only its cities lay in ruins; the people were bewildered by defeat.

The Japanese had firmly believed their country impregnable, sacred and inviolate. They had assumed that the same ' divine wind ' called *kamikaze* would overcome the enemy, as in the thirteenth century, when the Mongols had attacked their island with superior forces, and a typhoon had descended, scattering and destroying the mighty enemy fleet. The Japanese had never known defeat before; now they were an occupied country with a foreign power ruling them.

Strange as it may seem, the people showed no bitterness. They accepted that their country had erred—war was wrong. Ruth Benedict, in *The Chrysanthemum and the Sword* explains: 'Japan's real strength, which she can use in remaking herself into a peaceful nation, lies in her ability to say of a course of action, " That failed, " and then throw her energies into other channels. The Japanese have an ethic of alternatives.'

Five days after VJ Day, before an American had landed on Japan, the great Tokyo paper, the *Mainichi Shimbun*, could speak of defeat and of the political changes it would bring, saying: ' But it was all to the good for the ultimate salvation of Japan.' The editorial stressed that no one should for a moment forget that they had been completely defeated. Because their efforts to build up a Japan based on sheer might had met with utter failure, they must henceforth tread the path of a peaceful nation.

The *Asahi*, another great Tokyo newspaper, the same week characterized Japan's late ' excessive faith in military force ' as a ' serious error ' in its national and international policy. ' The old attitude, from which we could gain so little and suffered so much, should be discarded for a new one which is rooted in international co-operation and love of peace.'

The Japanese are essentially an honest people. Self-criticism is part of their make-up, and because they admitted war to be wrong and set their face to follow the path of peace, basing the rebuilding of their nation on truth, the foundation was solid and sure. No poison or festering sores of false self-justification were in their system; purged and purified they started to build a better Japan from the ruins that remained.

Soon after the end of hostilities a number of officers, Hasegawa among them, formed a Salvation Army Reconstruction Committee. A letter sent to General Albert Orsborn, who had succeeded General George Carpenter in 1946, expressed a desire that The Salvation Army be re-established as a separate organization, united to the international Salvation Army.

Meanwhile *Airinkai*, the social branch of The Salvation Army which had functioned throughout the war under the name ' Love to neighbour ', carried on rescue operations. Conditions in the cities were appalling; in place of homes and schools were rubble and craters; factories and bridges had become crumbling walls and phantom frames of twisted iron. Thousands were homeless, seeking shelter for the night in underground stations or living in ramshackle, makeshift huts.

On June 20, 1946, the General dispatched Brigadier Charles S. Davidson, as his personal representative, to investigate possibilities and negotiate with those in power. The Brigadier was familiar with Japanese conditions having previously served in the country.

Some twenty officers were called by the Brigadier to a private meeting at the Tsukishima Jijokan, where Lieut.-Commissioner Uyemura was reinstated Territorial Commander and a foundation laid for reconstruction.

Three months later, September 22, a public meeting was held at the city hall in Kanda, Tokyo. To this historic gathering former soldiers and officers, loyal to the Army, travelled from all parts of Japan. A few still had their uniforms intact; others improvised theirs. In this meeting the re-establishment of The Salvation Army in

Japan was formally announced. Many were the Hallelujahs and Amens!

With the rank of Lieut.-Colonel, Charles Davidson was appointed as Chief Secretary; Captain Hasegawa becoming the Colonel's secretary and translator.

To shelter some of the many homeless, a hostel was opened at Yokohama Minshukan. Feeding centres were set up in different parts of Tokyo. Food remained scarce long after the war had ended, particularly in the cities. Mrs. Hasegawa and the three children stayed in the country because Government restriction prohibited citizens moving into the city from rural areas. Not until eighteen months after the war were members of the family reunited in a home of their own.

A small incident about this time gives further insight to Hasegawa's character. A young Salvationist called at his office wanting to speak to him about future service. He recalls: ' It was lunch-time when I reached Headquarters and was shown into Captain Hasegawa's office. A piece of bread was lying on his table. After we had talked a little while, Captain Hasegawa said, " I am going to have lunch now, won't you have some with me? " And he broke the bread in two halves and handed me one. In those difficult days a piece of bread was precious and often the cause of quarrels in families. Hasegawa's half a piece of bread was spiritual food to me. There were many homeless orphans in the hills of Ueno in Tokyo where I lived. Once, one of these children begged from me some food which I was eating in the park. I could not give it then, so I stood up and ran away from that boy. When Captain Hasegawa gave me the bread I remembered my own experience and felt humiliated. I saw the strength and greatness of a man who had partaken of the Bread of Life who is Christ Jesus. I decided to follow his example and give my life in service for others as an officer in The Salvation Army.' Major Kuwahara has since rendered many years' service, both in corps and social institutions.

Rehabilitation work was carried out by officers using their own initiative whenever they saw a special need. Major Yamada and Captain Mikki, two women officers, noticing children left to roam the streets while mothers were at work, gathered the little ones in a park and cared for them until the mothers' return. It was December, not a time for open-air activities, the temperature near zero, but no indoor place could be found in the locality. The principal of a nearby primary school, impressed by what he saw, invited the officers to bring the children to the school where rooms were put at their disposal. This marked the beginning of a day nursery. Later, the Army built its own premises in Joto, a suburb of Tokyo, and the work with such a modest beginning has flourished.

The Major has gone to her heavenly reward and the Captain, up to her retirement ' mothered ' 150 children, all the while improving conditions and increasing equipment to a high standard. The children, from the age of three, do a three-year ' course ' after which they ' graduate '. Graduation is a very important occasion with mothers present wearing ceremonial kimono and the children, smiling and bowing, receiving their certificate in the form of a beautiful scroll.

Prince Takamatsu, younger brother of Emperor Hirohito, said in a speech about the Government's programme for social relief: ' What we need in this work, to give it true purpose and effect, is a spirit of religious zeal such as characterizes the work of The Salvation Army.'

A spirit of religious zeal is the motivating power of the Army's work. The gospel of Christ and service to needy mankind are interrelated. Man's need is not solely physical. In Japan, in those days, was a hunger no bread could satisfy. With evangelical work re-established in the cities and isolated villages, Salvationists preached Christ's gospel and His power to assuage man's spiritual hunger.

*Chapter
Ten*

AS AMBASSADOR

JAPAN is in many ways unique, a country of a single race speaking one language. In this it finds its strength, for there is strength in unity, and the people of Japan have prospered because of their unity. Not for them the wrangling of State autonomy caused by division of language, or the cult of individualism prevalent in the Occident. They have been satisfied to work for the common good of the country, in teams, putting their shoulders to the wheel, sharing the common burden of life.

Good as this may be, one can, however, in such a system detect a flaw. In a closed society made up of one race, the international spirit is likely to be found wanting. The Japanese are aware of this, as an editorial in the *Japan Times*, March 29, 1972 stated:

' The Economic Research Council recommends certain changes in the education system of Japan. The committee upholds the UNESCO 1961 image of the ideal man as being capable of " affection " and " considerateness ". But Japan's present educational system alone is not capable of producing such men. What is needed is a system of life-long education designed to enable an individual to develop his talents and individuality to the fullest and to participate in wide-ranging social activities embracing not only Japan, but the whole wide world.

' The committee criticizes the school system and hits at the parochialism of Japanese education and calls for greater internationalization of the nation's universities through both students and professors exchanges. It also recommends fundamental reforms in the present method of teaching foreign languages.'

Dr. Chie Nakane, a respected and eminent scholar, the only woman professor at the University of Tokyo, stated also in the *Japan Times*: 'Japan is still too isolated from other countries. In every major field are too few people who can really communicate. Every key person today should be international, able to deal internationally, but many of the *élite* do not even speak English.'

With the new prosperity has come a desire to see the world and break away from isolation. Within the last few years, to travel abroad is the ' done thing' for Japanese who can afford it. Many will spend all their savings on a trip to an overseas country—yet the isolation remains. With no means of communication, Japanese tourists move in groups, and one often reads in Japanese papers of the concern felt for the Japanese ' image ' abroad. Centuries of isolation from the rest of the world, inability to communicate through a common language and a natural inherited reserve and shyness, give a wrong impression of a most charming and courteous people and keep them within the barriers of their own isolation.

Hasegawa did all he could throughout his life-time to break down this barrier. He believed with the Indian sage Rabindranath Tagore: ' Universalism is not breaking down the walls of your house, but opening the door to your neighbours.'

Logic in the Far East works by laws often differing from western concepts. Anthropology divides man into different races, each with an intellectual constitution differing from the other. Due to this, misunderstandings may occur. We do not think alike; our ways of reasoning may differ. We do not, in fact, speak the same language metaphorically and literally. The first step toward understanding is to learn each other's language and here Hasegawa was a true mediator.

AS AMBASSADOR

The structure of the Japanese language is quite different from the English, and translating from English to Japanese and vice versa often creates problems. Japanese is essentially a written language, with characters borrowed from China, representing symbols rather than sounds. As there are many sounds with the same meaning, it is sometimes difficult in conversation to convey an exact meaning and not uncommon to see people, when wanting to make sure of a certain word, writing in the palm of their hand.

Two eminent statesmen, one Chinese, the other Japanese, recounted their experiences when meeting many years before in Tokyo as young students. The Chinese knew English but no Japanese, the Japanese knew neither Chinese nor English. Yet they found, to their amusement, they could converse, however faultily, by scribbling *kanjis* (Chinese characters) in their note-books and showing them to each other. Being symbols they convey the same meaning in both languages, even though the sound they represent is different.

To take a couple of very simple illustrations: the character for ' river ' is three vertical lines signifying the running water of a river. The word ' mouth ' is an open square. This is seen on railways stations, airports and other public buildings. Together with another character it signifies ' entrance ' or ' exit '; one just has to be sure of the other character so as not to go in the wrong direction. It does not take long before one learns the signs for ' airport ', ' station ', and so on, without actually being able to read; that is, without knowing the Japanese words for the signs.

In case all this sounds too easy, I will make amends by recording how I first learnt the extreme intricacy of the Japanese written language:

Two learned doctors sat on either side of me at a dinner party. To make small talk was difficult although my companions were bilingual. In ignorance I thought this a good opportunity to learn one or two Japanese words, and thus break the painful silence. I had heard the sound ' *ko* ' again and again, and it puzzled me; it seemed to be linked to so many words, sometimes preceding, sometimes ending, and sometimes on its own.

To the elderly gentleman on my right I said: ' Would you mind telling me the meaning of " *ko* "; it seems to be a very important word in your language.'

' I beg your pardon? '

I repeated my request.

' " *Ko* " did you say? Ah, *ko—ko—ko!* '

Putting his head on one side, he looked thoughtful and puzzled for a long time. Still no answer. He then turned to another elderly professor sitting on his right and asked the question in Japanese. Both of them started saying, ' *ko—ko—ko* ', drawing in their breath and making signs in the palms of their hands.

By now, completely mystified, I became more and more embarrassed. Why could they not give a simple answer to a perfectly simple question? Luckily there was an interruption—an after dinner speech—and ' *ko* ' was forgotten.

On returning home the first thing I did was to look up my newly acquired Japanese-English dictionary. No wonder there had been no easy answer! The question must have seemed utterly stupid to these Japanese friends. ' *Ko* ' and ' *Kō* ' can be written in no fewer than eighty-three different characters, each with a completely different meaning. Not so easy at all! How were my learned friends to know which ' *ko* ' I meant? If only I had been able to write it in the palm of my hand!

The language barrier often seems insurmountable; even when a Japanese has a fairly good knowledge of English, misunderstanding may occur. Frequently one gets ' no ' for an answer when one had expected ' yes '; this can be most confusing. Never ask a Japanese a question in the negative; or something like the following may result.

You say to him: 'Have you not been to England?'
He will answer 'No', although he has been.
'Oh, I thought you had been.'
Smilingly he will say: 'Yes, I have been.'
'But you said "No"!'
'No, no, no!' He puts up his hand in protest. He feels hurt that you should think he has not been to England when he has!

It takes a long time for a person from another land to understand that a Japanese will answer 'yes' or 'no' according to what you say is right or wrong, and if you ask if he has *not* been to England and he has—well, you are wrong, therefore he will say 'No', and he is perfectly right!

Plenty of English words are incorporated in the Japanese language, yet you are fortunate if you recognize them as such. In spite of having three different scripts with the thousands of Chinese characters, *Katagana* and *Hiragana*, there are in fact only twenty basic sounds. 'V' and 'L' are non-existent, so 'Vivian' becomes 'Bibian', 'collection' becomes 'correction' and when you 'fly' you 'fry'. Hearing of a little girl who came every day to 'pray' I was duly impressed, until I realized that like all little children she was spending her time in 'play'.

There are no consonants as such in the Japanese language; each sound must have a vowel following, except 'n' which occurs at the end of words: Sakamoto, Kageyama, Shimura, Hiramoto, Faji*n*. Therefore, when English words are used and transcribed in the Hiragana alphabet, used entirely for foreign words, each consonant is followed by a vowel: 'Christmas' becomes 'Kurisumasu', 'Table' is 'Teberu', 'Speed' on the motorways reads 'Supidu'.

Outside a magnificent building of modern architecture, in the holiday resort of Karuizawa, stood a name-plate carved in wood, as are most name-plates in the province. The name, written in Hiragana, indicated a foreign one. It read: ' *Ku-ra-bu* '. Was it the residence of a fabulously rich Mr. Crab? Later we discovered it to be the ' Club '.

Personally, I maintain it is more difficult for a Japanese to learn a western language than for a westerner to learn Japanese—at least spoken Japanese. As for learning to write it correctly, one would need a lifetime.

A main reason for Japanese insularity is doubtless the language barrier, for it is by help of words that we communicate, and when an abyss of silence exists between them and us, misunderstanding can so easily arise. How invaluable was a person like Hasegawa, born and bred a Japanese, yet understanding and appreciating the Occidental way of thinking and expression of language! Few Japanese read other than Japanese books. Hasegawa had the wider view. He read extensively in English and Japanese, and followed with keen interest Salvation Army world events through Army publications. He kept abreast of ideas and thoughts from other lands.

Even as a young Captain, at a time when learning a foreign language was not particularly popular in Japan, Hasegawa started classes in English in Kyobashi Corps in Tokyo. An ardent believer in the internationalism of The Salvation Army, he wanted his countrymen to learn English—to have a wider vision and to join hands with Salvationists around the world.

Akashi San, Corps Secretary of Kyobashi Corps, member of Territorial Headquarters Band, and holding a good position in Government, is one of many influenced by Hasegawa's English classes.

He recalled: ' I began to have contact with Captain Hasegawa before the war, when The Salvation Army had to change its name to *Kyu-sei-dan*. I owe him much, as I was taught by him Bible knowledge and English. My

AS AMBASSADOR

Commanding Officer was Captain Shinichi Yoshida (now Territorial Commander of Japan) and Hasegawa was also Captain then. He taught us English and the words from the Bible, and he was always kind, with a smile on his face. Many young people sought and found salvation. A songster brigade and youth group were organized. Young people were appointed local officers and the foundation of the corps was established. As a member of the Bible class, my faith was revived and I began to take part in the youth group activities. The young lady who became my wife was also one of Captain Hasegawa's students.'

She belonged to a family who followed the Nichiren doctrine. Followers of Nichiren are different from the otherwise tolerant and peace-loving Buddhists. They have taken their name after the founder of the sect who was a Buddhist priest, an intolerant fighter and fervent nationalist, who stirred the people to a frenzied zeal bordering on fanaticism.

Akashi San continued: 'At first my wife wanted to study English, but gradually she was influenced by Hasegawa's personality and led to the Christian faith.'

Both she and her husband have radiated a remarkable influence throughout many years in Army circles and beyond. She with her charming, friendly nature especially helped the women of the home league.

As a Salvation Army officer, Hasegawa visited England three times. The first occasion was in the summer of 1956, when he attended the International Corps Cadet Congress. Brigadier Hidetomo Koyano gives a delightful account of their experience, as he and Candidate Akiko Sakamoto (later Captain and Territorial Youth Secretary) accompanied Senior-Major Hasegawa to London.

The voyage was long, lasting fifty days, but when the sea was rough, the experienced sailor cheered his companions. They also depended on him to translate for them. Although both Koyano and Sakamoto had some knowledge of English, they found it, at that time, inadequate. However, when they sat down to their first meal on board ship, and were handed the menu card, it so happened Hasegawa let them down. Even *his* English, which they had believed perfect, seemed not to meet the present requirement. In a double sense he was completely at sea!

At the next meal he brought his English dictionary. With the menu in one hand and the dictionary in the other, he tried to give the order, yet without success. The menu was in French!

But, if French was beyond him, he understood and appreciated London wit. He and his companions were standing in a long queue waiting for a bus. It was rush hour; many buses were full, and did not halt. When eventually one stopped, in which there was room for only one more passenger, the conductor shouted: ' One—good! ' With typical London humour a man, second in the queue, called back: ' Too (two) bad! ' Everybody, including Hasegawa, thought it a good joke and, for a moment, the long minutes of weary waiting were forgotten.

Hasegawa remained in England for six months during his 1956 visit. After the Corps Cadet Congress he went to the International Training College to observe the methods in training young people for Salvation Army officership. In February of the previous year he had been appointed Training Principal of the college in Tokyo, and to observe training methods in the motherland of The Salvation Army was of considerable value. In spite of the great distance between the two countries, similarities between the college in England and the college in Japan were many. He found the same discipline, the same practical training in evangelism, the same fervour and devotion in the young people dedicated to a life of self-sacrifice and service—an astounding fact of unity between

AS AMBASSADOR

Salvationists right round the world! Hindu, Buddhist, Shintoist, Moslem and the unconverted in 'Christian' lands, all become one when the miracle of God's saving grace, through Jesus Christ, reaches them. There is no longer East or West but one unity in Christ.

His second visit occurred in June 1965 when he and other Salvationists from Japan attended The Salvation Army's Centenary Celebrations in London. Then Lieut.-Commissioner and Territorial Commander for Japan, he was a most worthy representative of his country. Back in his homeland he gave his people impressions of wonderful events, describing in graphic word pictures the large gatherings in the Royal Albert Hall, especially that graced by the presence of Her Majesty Queen Elizabeth the Second. He made his audiences in distant Japan feel the solemnity of the occasion when the bust of William Booth was unveiled in Westminster Abbey. He told them of the moving sight as hundreds of people came forward to rededicate themselves to God in the final meeting of the celebrations. Not only did Hasegawa represent Japan to the West; he also represented the international Salvation Army to his homeland.

The Commissioner's last visit to the United Kingdom was four years later, as member of the High Council (prior to the retirement of General Frederick Coutts) for the election of Erik Wickberg as ninth General of The Salvation Army. Failing health had necessitated his relinquishing the position of Territorial Commander, but his wise counsel was of immense value to Commissioner Theo. Holbrook who, as a retired officer, for a few months carried responsibility for the territory, as well as to the incoming Territorial Commander, Lieut.-Commissioner Don Smith.

On his final journey to England Mrs. Hasegawa accompanied her husband, ever watchful over his health and ensuring he followed doctor's orders. She endeared herself, by her vivacity and high spirits, to all whom they met during this visit. They found great joy in seeing old friends who had earlier served in Japan. Friendships once formed were not forgotten.

On their return journey they travelled *via* America and visited also the home, in Hawaii, of the Commissioner's elder sister, Suga San, chief instrument in leading the young naval cadet to Christ and who, throughout his life, had had a strong influence upon him.

As a young officer Suga San had left Tokyo to marry a Japanese Salvation Army officer in Hawaii. There she served with her husband, Captain Soichi Ozaki, for some years. On returning to an appointment in Japan their little son was killed by the truck taking their luggage to the ship. A couple of years later they sailed for Korea, where, a few months after, Adjutant Ozaki was promoted to Glory.

With her young daughter, Suga San returned to Japan. As a widow she held important positions at headquarters and in social institutions, before moving in retirement to Hawaii to live with her daughter, who had married and settled there.

With great joy the eighty-one-year-old sister received her younger brother and his wife into her home. Looking back over the years, she thanked God for His leadings and the part her brother had been allowed to play in the history of The Salvation Army in Japan, undreamed of when as a young lad he gave himself to God in Kanda Corps hall.

In a land where English is little known and many Salvationists are new to the Christian faith, books explaining Army doctrines in the language of the country are of great importance. In translating the *Handbook of Doctrine* from English to Japanese, Commissioner Hasegawa probably rendered some of his most valuable work. His translation was of the highest order, and when, in

1965, the first translation of *The Soldier's Armoury* was published, this was welcomed and read by Salvationists and church-members alike. He also translated a number of widely-used songs.

During General Wickberg's visit to Japan in 1970, the Commissioner, then in his seventieth year and frail in body, translated the General's addresses in every meeting and, though often feeling exhausted with the tremendous mental strain, there was never any slackening. In constant and sustained alertness, he carried on masterfully and buoyantly translating throughout the campaign.

A truly wonderful interpreter, merging his own personality with the speaker, until there seemed but one voice, yet Hasegawa's finest translation was of God's word lived out unceasingly in his own saintly life.

Chapter
Eleven

AS AN EVANGELIST

As the memory of war receded into the past, a new era started for Japan. With energy, determination and diligence, marked characteristics of the people, they set themselves to raise, from the ashes, a new Japan. They rebuilt their cities and factories. By 1950, pre-war level of production had been surpassed. In 1964 Japan's Gross National Product was the fifth largest in the world and in 1968 Japan ranked as the world's third richest nation.

This meant an improvement in living standards. While housing, for a large majority, remains the same, with limited space, rooms measured by the size of *tatami* mats, sparsely furnished, on *tatami* floors now stand colour television sets giving a choice of twelve programmes, almost round the clock. Kitchens are equipped with electric refrigerators, washing machines and automatic rice cookers.

A better economy enables freedom of movement; the wife is no longer marooned in the kitchen; friends are entertained at restaurants. Occasionally, the family has a festive meal out, where the children behave with accustomed decorum.

Eating habits have changed; meat often takes the place of fish, many varieties of imported food are available. The younger generation is taller than the parents. People are well dressed; it seems as though they always wear new clothes. One never sees a child that is dirty or shabbily dressed.

Husband and wife enjoy equality under the law, with equal rights in contracting marriage, in inheriting and owning property, and in suing for divorce. Parental rights are absolutely equal in the educating and upbringing of their children, as opposed to the pre-war system by which the father had greater authority under the law.

Shorter working hours give more time for relaxation, although many people still have only one free Saturday in the month. More and more motor vehicles make driving a nightmare. To ease traffic transportation, networks of super-motorways are constantly expanded; elevated motorways with fly-over upon fly-over have been built in Tokyo and the larger cities, till man feels like a midget in a vast forest of concrete pillars.

Pollution is the country's greatest problem; rows upon rows of cherry-blossom trees have lost their delicate hues in Tokyo's congested streets. To breathe fresh mountain air people go in groups to the country, sometimes with a guide carrying a flag. Fast trains, leaving Tokyo every few minutes, are crowded yet always orderly. During winter months skis are lined up on racks and young people spend week-ends or a Sunday at hotels in the mountains.

Many travel abroad during holidays, to see how other people live, to measure their own standards with others, to learn new ways, to find out whether people of other lands have found the secret of contentment through purposeful living.

The Japanese should have pride and confidence from their economic achievement, but in many hearts are feelings of doubt and bewilderment, and the question where will it lead them? They fear the fast-moving industrialization which on the one hand has brought the country prosperity, while on the other hand, environmental pollution and overcrowding in cities, without giving any sense of security and contentment.

In an article, 'Toward a better understanding of my country', Kyozo Mori says: 'Since the end of world war two, Japan has stood for " peace and democracy." Under this slogan what Japan has actually done is to raise its Gross National Product. But its efforts have proved to be another short-circuit thinking. Today the Japanese people are harassed by the question, " What is the purpose of our feverish economic activity anyway? " They are now groping for salvation in the traditional Shinto way of thinking—that is, to live in, or as part of, nature rather than confronting nature, and in the Buddhist way of thinking that everything transmigrates in the natural world as well as in man's world.'

Hasegawa saw the spiritual vacuum of his people and was oppressed by the plight of those who did not know the true God. In possession of the secret of purposeful living he knew the source of true joy, and his one passion was to share it with others.

As Training Principal, a position he held for four and a half years, he had opportunity to meet and influence many people. Young men, feeling emptiness within themselves, came to him and inquired about the Christian religion. Patiently and with conviction, he explained to them the great truths as seen from his own experience.

He found supreme satisfaction in training cadets for Army service and infused them with capacity for love, ever reminding them of the Master's words: ' Continue ye in My love.' Many present-day officers remember him as father-like, sympathetic and understanding, helping them strive toward the highest. He prayed with the cadets before they went out on practical work—house-visiting, *War Cry* selling, teaching the children—and joined them in open-air meetings, preaching the gospel of redemption through Christ.

To a cadet returning worried to the college with papers unsold, he said encouragingly: ' Don't be disappointed, even though you have not done well at the present stage. If you were to succeed at everything there would be no need for training! You will find it gets easier gradually.

AS AN EVANGELIST

Just be sure not to lose your spiritual glow.' After that the cadet accepted happily whatever task was set her.

Often he spoke to them of holiness: a quality of life so clearly expressed in his daily living. Remembering his own call to officership, he would remind them of Jesus' words to Peter: ' Simon, son of Jonas, lovest thou Me more than these? ' And the cadets would feel a strange power in the words spoken, as their hearts filled with longing for greater and more perfect love. When Major Hasegawa asked them to join in singing his favourite song, they would respond in a spirit of dedication and self-surrender:

> All in my heart, Lord, Thou canst read;
> Master, Thou knowest I love Thee indeed.
> Ask what Thou wilt my devotion to test,
> I will surrender the dearest and best.

Later, as Field Secretary, responsible for evangelistic work, he travelled the length and breadth of Japan preaching the gospel, inspiring officers and soldiers. Sensitive to the needs of his officers, many of whom were working alone in remote villages, he understood their peculiar difficulties; his own encounter with ill-health making him sympathetic, when weariness and fatigue beset them. He implored them to be patient, a virtue he himself practised and had mastered. He could speak out of his own sufferings and a letter or sympathetic word helped many on the brink of giving up.

A young woman Lieutenant stationed at Kobe Corps—her Captain was on the verge of leaving her work—felt burdened and discouraged. When she received her corrected probationary lessons from Headquarters she saw in Brigadier Hasegawa's handwriting: ' Call upon me in the day of trouble. I will deliver thee.' ' I knew he could not write direct to me,' recalls the officer, ' so he encouraged me with the words written on my lessons. I was grateful for his kindness, it helped me to stand firm.'

Travelling from corps to corps was often tough going. Some meetings were poorly attended. Fully aware that officers stationed in small corps among people indifferent to the Christian gospel carried the heavier burden, he was constantly at their side to help them in their task.

Visiting Wakamatsu in Tohoku Division one winter's day, snow-clad mountains towering above the little town and cold wind blowing, Hasegawa left the train and, accompanied by the Commanding Officer who met him, went to the corps hall. A salvation meeting had been announced. It was a week-day and people were still at work. Undaunted, Hasegawa suggested they should hold an open-air meeting. The snow lay thick on the ground when the Brigadier, the Captain and the Lieutenant took their stand on a corner of the street, proclaiming the gospel of Christ as Saviour of the world. The Captain and Lieutenant played their cornets, the Brigadier beat the drum. When the meeting was over, the Captain started to walk back but Hasegawa said, 'Let's march!' and off they marched through the narrow shopping streets festooned with paper flowers. That night more people than usual attended the salvation meeting and some were converted.

Three years later, at the end of 1962, Lieut.-Colonel Hasegawa became Chief Secretary, second in command of Japan. On one occasion, while visiting the northern island of Hokkaido, he was suddenly recalled to Tokyo. After boarding the ship to take him to the main island of Honshu, the officer at the port town received a message for Hasegawa from the Territorial Commander. Rushing on to the boat he looked for the Chief Secretary in the first-class cabins. He was not there. The officer recalls: 'I thought, as the Colonel had been very tired, he must be resting in a sleeping cabin. I asked one of the stewards to look for him, but he could not find him. At last I went down to the bottom of the ship and found the Colonel

AS AN EVANGELIST

sitting talking to the people who carried illegal goods—mainly rice and beans—commodities which were scarce in those days. After giving the message I said to the Colonel: " It is dark here. I know you are tired. Won't you have a cabin where you can rest? "

' He answered, " I am used to the boat and I love this part of the ship best." He smiled, then, turning to his travel companions carrying the illegal goods, he continued his conversation. In Colonel Hasegawa I could see the face of the Apostle Paul as he travelled with the gospel to Macedonia, in Europe, across the Aegean Sea. Ten years have passed since then. When I think of Commissioner Hasegawa, the true evangelist, his fine figure on the platform does not come to me; but the stooped figure, sitting in the dark at the bottom of the ship, telling the travellers of the love of God.'

In November, 1964, he was appointed Territorial Commander for Japan. On receiving the cable from the General in London, Hasegawa's first action was to go to the hall in Kanda and there kneel at the Mercy Seat, where forty-eight years earlier, as a young student, he had knelt giving himself to God to be used for His Kingdom. Here, spreading out the cable before the Lord and rededicating himself to God's will and purpose he claimed divine grace and wisdom for the onerous task which lay before him.

Administration work made heavy demands upon his time, yet his greatest concern was, as ever, that the people of Japan should come to know the true God and that the officers should maintain a passion for soul-saving work, that their love for God and their fellow men be kept warm and vital. At a Brengle Institute at Tozanso, where the doctrine of holiness was reaffirmed and officers spent time in meditation and Bible study, it was suggested that morning prayers on the last day be held on the hillside. The mountains around were bathed in morning mist; then the sun arose, a golden orb on the far horizon. Commissioner

Hasegawa invited the officers, if they felt so led, to join hands as a symbol of love and, as the sun rose higher and all were united, he prayed that an outpouring of the Holy Spirit might fill them with the same love as possessed their Master.

During Hasegawa's term as Territorial Commander, Government sponsored a television programme on Gunpei Yamamuro, marking the twenty-fifth anniversary of his death. Nearly an hour was given to portraying the life and work of the first Japanese Salvation Army officer, who also became the first oriental Commissioner. Yamamuro's prayer as a young Christian, that he be enabled to convey the message of the gospel in a language understood by all, and write the truth in a way that anyone could read and be enlightened, had been amply fulfilled. His *Common People's Gospel*, completed while on honeymoon, had been read by millions the length and breadth of Japan. And one who had listened to his words was now the leader of the Army in Japan, carrying the gospel message far and wide.

After four and a half years, sickness made necessary his relinquishing the position of Territorial Commander. He then took office as Territorial Counsellor, sharing his many years' experience, never enforcing his opinion, yet graciously and courteously offering advice. Most of his time was now devoted to translation work.

When the Commissioner had finally to lay down his pen, his daughter, Mrs. Captain Kazuko Harita, also an accomplished linguist, took over the exacting task of translating *The Soldier's Armoury*, and the work, so dear to her father, continues. On August 12 1970, Hasegawa reached his seventieth year and, two months after, entered retirement. In his final farewell meeting, held at Tenma Corps in Osaka, he spoke of three women who had influenced his life: his mother, his sister Suga San, and his wife. Turning to Mrs. Hasegawa he said: ' I have

AS AN EVANGELIST

never really expressed my gratitude to you. Thank you, *Okachan* (Mama)!'

This brought forth laughter, a laughter accompanied by tears. Not often do the Japanese show their inmost feelings. For this human touch the Commissioner was revered even more than for his brilliant leadership.

At the close of this meeting all joined in singing:

> There's a land that is fairer than day,
> And by faith we can see it afar;
> For the Father waits over the way
> To prepare us a dwelling-place there.

It was Hasegawa's last public meeting. After returning from Osaka, he visited the Commanding Officer of Kanda Corps, where he was a soldier. He had come to pay for *The War Cry* and give his monthly cartridge (offering). He looked tired and sat down immediately he entered the officers' quarters.

The following day, in the evening, when crossing the street in front of the Evangeline Hall, where he was to attend the united holiness meeting, the accident occurred that ultimately claimed his life, and Hasegawa's soul was taken to the dwelling place prepared in the land that is fairer than day.

Not long after her husband's promotion to Glory, Mrs. Hasegawa sat turning the pages of his Bible. Among the leaves was a piece of paper. She unfolded it. It was headed 'My Will'. She read it carefully.

'A right relationship to God and our fellow men,' she read, 'To parents and children, brothers and sisters, husband and wife, superior officers and assisting officers, colleagues and comrades. The right relationship to those in our care: love them, lead them, make every effort for them; shed your tears for them many times. We are called to do it, we stake our lives for it.'

The document finished with: 'Take your share of suffering as a good soldier of Christ Jesus. Preach the word, be urgent in season and out of season, convince, rebuke and exhort, be unfailing in patience and in teaching.'

Hasegawa's ' will ' was to do the will of God. He had a burning desire that his countrymen should do the same. Mrs. Hasegawa knew this, so in her usual practical way had ' the will ' copied and sent to officers and soldiers alike that they might have a share in the ' will ' and help to build God's kingdom of love and peace in Japan.